What Society Does to Girls

Joyce Nicholson

Illustrated by
Mary Leunig

First published by
VIRAGO PRESS 1977
41 William IV Street
London WC2N 4DB

Second edition published by
Virago Limited 1980

Reprinted 1984, 1986

First published in Australia by
Pitman Publishing Pty Ltd

British Library Cataloguing in Publication Data
Nicholson, Joyce
    What society does to girls.—2nd ed.
    1. Sex role—England
    I. Title
    305.'0942   HQ1075.5.G7
    ISBN 0-86068-021-5

Printed in Great Britain by
Anchor Brendon Ltd, Tiptree, Essex

The author and publishers would like to thank
Rondor Music (London) Ltd,
147 Oxford Street, London W1R 1TB
for permission to quote from 'I Am a Woman' by Helen Reddy

CONTENTS

1   Having My Eyes Opened 5-7

2   Early Conditioning 8-15

3   Equality of Education? 16-25

4   The Conflict of Conforming 26-36

5   The Mirage of Marriage 37-49

6   Man-made Myths 50-56

7   The Double Standard 57-64

8   What Are the Solutions? 65-67

9   A Final Word for Girls 68

10 Read On 69-71

This witty and informative book is a lucid introduction to conditioning in our society. Written for young people as well as their parents and teachers, it shows how, even in the 70s and 80s, society has restricted choices and opportunities for development by too much conformity in upbringing, education and beliefs, both at home and at school.

Through her own and others' experiences, Joyce Nicholson analyses how girls are encouraged from birth to be passive rather than active, supportive rather than creative, and how their abilities are continually directed towards the personal and the domestic. To do this, she looks at education, marriage, work, myths about women, the double standard, and many other topics, and shows how girls' personalities are often moulded into a distorted. 'feminine' image, boys' into a 'masculine' one — to the detriment of both. Her conclusions point to ways in which girls and boys can change their situation to the benefit of everyone.

1 HAVING MY EYES OPENED

When I read *The Female Eunuch* by Germaine Greer, I could not sleep for three nights. I felt she must have taken me as a case history, and so much that I had not been able to understand was suddenly made clear.

I had for a long time been aware of discrimination and unfair attitudes towards women. I had been conscious that a woman always had to do something much better than a man to get an equal reward. I had noticed that a sane and sensible remark by a woman, in a group, went unnoticed, but the same remark by a man was immediately taken up as a good contribution to the conversation. When I saw a point more quickly than some men in important positions, I knew I often had to curb my tongue and show great patience whilst waiting for them to mentally catch up to me. There were plenty of men, of course, who were mentally ahead of me.

At the same time there were many things I did not understand. Why did I get more nervous than men when speaking in public? Why did I have to admit many women were far more foolish and silly than men? Why did girls burst into tears? Why were there no great women inventors, few women painters or composers? It had often puzzled me.

I felt sure that women were equal to men. They were often more logical than men, yet there were other situations where they did appear different and inferior.

I knew a great deal about early discriminations against women. I remember my feelings of disbelief about the injustices visited upon women in the last century. I think I have always been disturbed by injustice of any kind, and to learn that, until the passing of the Married Women's Property Act in 1870, women lost all control over their money when they married had filled me with anger. To quote Kate Millett in *Sexual Politics:*

> Under the common law which prevailed in both countries (England and USA) at the opening of the period, a woman underwent 'civil death' upon marriage, forfeiting what amounted to every human right, as felons now do upon entering prison...
> Her husband became something like a legal keeper, as by marrying she succumbed to a mortifying process which placed her in the same class with lunatics or idiots, who were also 'dead in the law'.

The history of that time is filled with very sad stories of men marrying heiresses, going through their fortunes, and leaving them destitute. Women such as Edith Nesbitt, the author of the wonderful Bastable books, kept writing against great odds, only to have her libertine husband spend all the money she earned.

I had read widely about the battle the suffragettes waged at the end of the last century and the beginning of this to obtain votes for women, how they tied themselves to railings, burnt mail in letter boxes, and, when they were sent to jail, went on hunger strikes and suffered forced feeding. One actually threw herself under a race horse and was killed.

I even wrote a junior novel about a young girl in the 1890s and her struggle against an autocratic father to be allowed to go to school and then to study medicine at the university, and into the story I brought the battle that women had throughout the world to be accepted in the medical profession. For many years women were not allowed to work as doctors in hospitals. In 1978, 81.1 per cent of the hopsital doctors in Britain were men, 18.9 per cent women. Only 14.8 per cent of general practitioners in Britain in the same year were women. Up to the passing of the Sex Discrimination Act in 1975 there was still a strict quota system operating for women in most medical schools. In America the figures for 1977 showed that only 9.85 per cent of doctors were women. In Australia the first time a women medical student came top of her year at Melbourne University she was not allowed to go to the Melbourne Hospital, where the top men students always went for further practical study. The first women doctors in Melbourne were not allowed to operate in the established hopsitals, and had to build their own hospital.

My researches into this subject meant I *knew* women could be as clever as men, even in the sciences and mathematics, those subjects considered unsuitable for women.

But this still left unanswered the problem of why so many girls and women giggled or laughed too loudly, cried, talked nonsense, did not interest themselves in politics, did not try at sport, were unreliable and silly, did, in fact, often appear inferior to the majority of men. The truth was that although I often wondered about these things, and formed my own unsatisfactory theories, my reading about feminism and women's rights stopped when they won the right to vote. In fact, it stopped in the same way that feminism itself stopped once women got the vote. Two world wars and a depression had taken away the militancy from feminism, had driven them to home-making and mothering, so that they did not learn how to use that vote.

I was unaware of the second wave of feminism, when women began again to realise that they were still deprived in many respects. They had obtained the vote, they had done away with the greatest legal disabilities against them, but they still held very few top positions, there were still few women politicians, they were seldom found in places of power where the great decisions were made. They were still almost as entrapped as ever, still economically dependent on men, and frequently battling with large families because of the lack of control over their own bodies.

An easy answer to this is that because women physically bear the babies, they are necessarily unable to occupy the higher positions, and are forced out of the best positions in the workforce. But this is no real answer. It leaves unanswered the fact that unmarried women or women without children are also found in lower positions, or that a few women, a very few, with children, even with large families, have always managed to become professors, doctors, politicians and manage large companies. The odds have been against them, but they have managed it satisfactorily, without sacrificing their children or losing their so-called 'feminine' characteristics. So I knew there must be other solutions.

The second wave of feminism started, with Betty Friedan and others, at a time when I was still too busy battling with domestic chores and trying to solve my own personal problem of identity to be conscious of what was happening elsewhere. This was why it was not until the publication of *The Female Eunuch* in 1970 that a whole new world of thought and action was opened up to me.

Here I read for the first time the reasons why women are inferior in many ways. I read about conditioning, about how girls are trained from birth, by their parents, their peers and society, to be passive, to be mothers, to be supportive, actually to look foolish deliberately in order to be popular with boys, and how, at the age of puberty, when a boy's creativity is encouraged and grows stronger, a girl's creativity is taken away from her, and thus withers.

I lay in bed, I walked round the house in a daze, thinking over my life, and seeing how, at every stage, in so many things I had done, or attempted to do, this conditioning had been applied to me. Thankfully, as it turned out, particular traits in my character or lucky events had helped me to overcome some of my female conditioning and training.

In the following chapters I shall attempt to describe in personal terms, and in general terms, what conditioning did to me, what it does to girls, and what members of the feminist or women's movement and others are now doing to try and combat this influence.

2 EARLY CONDITIONING

From the moment the nurse in the hospital wraps a blue blanket around a baby boy and a pink blanket around a baby girl, boys and girls are treated differently by their parents, their relatives, their friends (or peers), the education system and society. Different things are expected of them. They get rewards for different forms of behaviour. They are encouraged to do different things. Is it any wonder they turn out differently?

You think these are extreme statements? Let us look at them more closely.

The way boys and girls develop is the result of two factors, their inherited characteristics and their upbringing. The greatest scientists and psychologists have not yet been able to work out where one begins and the other ends. There is frequent discussion about delinquents. Were they born bad or was it the result of their early upbringing, their environment?

Everyone accepts the fact that both inheritance and environment are of the greatest importance, and no one has ever been able to prove satisfactorily that there is any basic difference between the inherited intellectual qualities of men and women. Many people have tried, and if they could produce statistical evidence surely those in whose interest it is to keep women in an inferior position would present their evidence. But they have not produced it for they cannot produce it. There are no adequate facts to back their argument.

On the other hand, there are plenty of figures to show that women can be just as clever as men. Girls in the top classes do marginally better than boys, and although far more boys than girls stay at school for these grades, the rate of passes for girls is higher than for boys. More boys do scientific subjects than girls, but among the girls that study in these areas, more girls than boys get the top grades.

Apart from it being impossible to prove intellectual differences between male and female, it is also difficult to produce proofs of any absolute differences, other than physical, in their other characteristics.

Many men are born and grow up with so-called 'feminine' traits. They like cooking. They like looking after children. They like dressmaking, hairdressing, nursing, colourful clothes, all those things usually associated with women.

Many women are born with so-called 'masculine' traits. As little girls they are known as 'tomboys'. They grow up and ride motorbikes or drive fast cars; they are sometimes aggressive in their manner; they even, given the opportunity, make good managers. Some have clear, logical brains; they come top of their year in mixed classes in medicine and sciences, as well as in the so-called 'feminine' fields of arts, languages and the humanities.

In many cases therefore it can be seen that the line between the sexes is very narrow. In other cases it is as wide as the mouth of the River Amazon. Why do girls, with so much inherent ability, so often end up in lowly-paid positions, in supportive, assisting roles, such as secretary, nurse, air hostess, while the men become managers, doctors, airline pilots?

Let us go back to those blue and pink blankets. The baby, wrapped in those blankets, will probably go home to blue jackets for boys and pink jackets for girls, blue ribbons in the baby boy's

9

bootees, pink ribbons in the little girl's hair. If you see a very young baby wearing yellow clothes, he or she is probably the offspring of a conscious feminist mother, determined not to sex type her child from his or her first years. But the blue and the pink are only the outward signs of the belief among adults that boys and girls are different.

From the moment the baby is conscious of the reactions of adults to him or her, he or she learns that different actions get different results and different rewards. Adults in a small child's life are of supreme importance. Children are completely dependent on them. They are the source of all things, good or bad, so children soon learn to do what pleases those all-important people and brings the wanted rewards.

The baby girl who is pretty, who smiles sweetly at her father, who grips his finger clingingly, will be looked at lovingly by him, may be picked up and hugged. The baby boy who kicks his legs strongly, waves his hands around with great vigour, even cries loudly, equally delights his father, and brings forth approving noises and an extra hug.

The toddling boy who makes loud booming noises, who knocks things over, who pushes along a toy car with great vigour, who even gets his clothes dirty, will equally win his parent's approval. 'Isn't he just like a little boy?' 'A real little boy, isn't he?' 'You can tell he's a boy, can't you?' But what happens to the little girl who makes booming, zooming noises, or who stands on her head, or throws a ball hard across the room? She is immediately aware she has done the wrong thing. Her father frowns, or pushes her away from him. Her mother or aunt or grandma is often equally critical. 'That's too rough for little girls'. 'Little girls don't get their dresses dirty.' 'You must sit still and be a little lady.'

You don't believe me? Do an exercise in listening and studying. It is quite fascinating, once you start to notice, to find out how often exactly the same action from a little boy or a little girl will bring a completely different reaction from an adult. If animals can be trained to do certain things to get certain rewards, how much easier to train a little boy or girl, who have far greater intelligence, and who early learn what brings them the best rewards.

A little girl cries, or wheedles, or looks up lovingly at her father, and father goes to her rescue or gives her what she wants. A little boy cries, and is told: 'Don't be a sissy' or 'Little boys don't cry.' He soon finds out that he earns disapproval for this type of behaviour and learns to face problems without crying, just as a little girl learns that roughness or toughness brings similar disapproval, and so curbs such behaviour.

I personally do not believe it is any more 'natural' for all little girls to be passive and quite, sweet and kind and clean, than it is 'natural'

for all little boys to be aggressive and creative, competitive, tough and masterful, the boss. Both things are taught to them at a very early age.

Take a look at children's toys. I have in front of me the Christmas catalogue of a famous department store. The head of page 1 is

TALKING, WALKING, FLOPPY, DRESSY:
SEE HUNDREDS OF DOLLS

Needless to say, a girl is pictured, among a collection of nine dolls. Out of the nine dolls, two are bride dolls and four are baby dolls. Is it any wonder that girls grow up to think their role in life is to be a bride and a mother?

Have you ever seen a bridegroom doll advertised for little boys, or a picture of a boy nursing a baby doll? At the bottom of the page there are three obviously male dolls. How are they dressed? One is an abominable snowman, one a soldier with a machine gun, and the third an explorer, also with a gun. So the image of the sort of people boys should be when they grow up is established just as early.

On page 3 of this catalogue, we find a toy headphone transistor radio. Who is wearing it? A little boy, of course, because boys are expected to understand mechanical, technical things. Page 5 features

EVERYTHING FOR BUSY LITTLE GIRLS
THE BIGGEST RANGE!

There is a toy sewing machine, with a little girl looking at it longingly (is it any wonder women comprise all the main machinists in clothing factories?), a toy ironing table, a vacuum cleaner, a clothes line, toy saucepans, a stove, a toy electric mixer, and a toy house, again featuring a smiling, happy girl. Does anyone ever suggest giving, or ever give, a boy any of these toys? Yet what law ordains that girls should wash and spin, and boys should not?

Ah, but pages 6 and 7, what do they feature? There are painting sets, a tool kit, a giant digger (heavy gauge metal), Meccano sets, a jumbo loader (in metal), and model railway with the caption 'the boy's first railway set', dumper trucks, a jumbo truck, a Land Rover, Lego buildings, a heavy tank, a chunky loader (heavy gauge metal) and a giant bulldozer. And who is playing with these toys? A small, smiling boy. Not only is a boy thus encouraged to play with mechanical tough toys, for these toys are given only to little boys, but note the words 'heavy', 'jumbo', 'giant', 'chunky' — all the qualities society thinks and says boys should have and be.

As soon as they can walk little girls tend to be dressed in pretty clothes, their hair is cut or curled or tied in a special way, with pretty ribbons, or washed with special shampoo. Girls are given toy make-up sets so they learn early it is important how they look — and to look artificial.

Advertisements are another strong conditioning factor. The ones which advertise shampoos and soaps stress prettiness or femininity in the hair or the clothes of girls. Little girls always have soft hair, soft skin, are pretty and sweet. But boys are shown in sturdy, often dirty clothes. In soap advertisements, mothers look with good-humoured despair at their sons' dirty clothes. They don't blame the boys. In fact, they are rather proud of them. They just bless the soap that will help them get the muddy clothes clean. Is it any wonder that little girls grow up thinking they must be pretty to gain rewards, attention and friends, and that outward things such as clothes are all-important? It is surprising that boys gain the impression that the important thing is to be themselves, that courage, activity, aggressiveness are the main things in life, irrespective of what happens to their clothes or their appearance? Mum will fix that up.

Yet, in fact, many little boys love pretty clothes, and don't really want to be tough, dirty little footballers. It is not only the girls who suffer. One wonders what agony generations of little boys have suffered through not being able to cry, having to be brave, not being allowed to play with dolls. Boys are usually discouraged from doing so-called 'feminine' things they may want to do. Did you know that only 8.3 per cent of nurses in Britain are men and that men were not allowed to be nurses in Australia until 1974? Did you realise that in Britain and Australia there are many more women than men in primary teaching, this being a job associated with caring for small children? In Britain in 1977, the percentage of women in primary school teaching was 87.8 per cent. Yet many men like teaching small children, but the higher financial rewards go to secondary teachers, so men, being taught to be ambitious, feel they must aim for secondary teaching.

Although I knew nothing of the theory of feminism or female or male conditioning until I read Germaine Greer, I always, in bringing up my own children, had a strong instinct that children should be allowed to be themselves, to be encouraged to do what they wanted to do. After all, the whole of modern educational theory is aimed at encouraging children to do their own thing at their own rate. I can therefore distinctly remember getting very angry at someone who told my eldest son, then seven years old, 'not to be a sissy'. He was sewing clothes to dress one of his toy animals.

That son is now a successful political cartoonist, and, perhaps, had I stopped him playing at dressing dolls and animals, he would not be nearly as creative. Who knows? He is also one of the younger generation who believes that men should share in the rearing of their children, and he very much shares in caring for his own three children. My father, also, had a great part in my childhood. He always put me to bed, always doctored me when I was sick, and helped my mother greatly with the housework. So you see how mixed up is the upbringing of us all. Although both my mother and father, I now realise, strongly conditioned me towards a 'feminine' role in many ways, there were other aspects of my upbringing which acted against this. That is why I feel like a case history for Germaine Greer's book. I can see where I was conditioned and greatly influenced to follow a typical female role, but I can see where other factors influenced me in other ways.

To return to the typical small boy and girl, we can see how in their toys and birthday cards, in the advertising that bombards us all the time, in the attitudes of parents and friends, we have the beginning of children's conditioning. Girls do quiet, passive, mothering things, helping in the house. Boys do aggressive, active, creative things. Girls appear as perfect little, sweet, characterless beings. Boys are full of character, leaders, tough, rough, even dirty, provided they achieve.

Do not think it is all black and white. Many parents do buy creative toys for girls. Many parents do teach little boys to be helpful in the house, gentle and loving. Also the inherited characteristics of many children are so strong that they overcome early influences, and in spite of all the toys, adult and society attitudes and actions, some boys grow up to be hairdressers and dressmakers, and some girls grow up to be scientists and to race cars. Also things are changing. People are learning about the conditioning that goes on.

But the facts are there. Against the odd parent or teacher who is aware, there is the mass of shops, advertisers, books, teachers, manufacturers, all steadily working to sex type children from the moment they are born. The overall picture, the overall weight of influence, is hard for boys and girls to overcome. It is particularly hard for a little girl, not born with either strong so-called 'feminine' or 'masculine' characteristics, to resist the pressure and grow up other than a typical female. Although she may not be basically 'feminine' any more than an average boy, unless she has a very strong, aggressive character, she is not really given a freedom of choice.

She is set in her ultimate role from babyhood, and it is not one she would necessarily choose.

SUGGESTIONS FOR OBSERVATION AND DISCUSSION

During the next few weeks, listen and look and collect information on the following:

1 See how often someone says, when a boy is rough, or tough, or dirty something like: 'Isn't that just like a boy!', and how often a girl is told she's not a proper girl or not ladylike because she's noisy, rough, or grubby.

2 Go into a newsagent's and study children's birthday cards. Collect descriptions of what boys and girls are doing on their cards.

3 Study children's toys. Make a list of the toys little girls are given and play with, and the toys little boys are given and play with. Study advertisements in the newspapers of toys for boys and girls. Make a list of those which are indicated as boys' toys, by illustration or words. List those which are indicated as girls' toys by illustration or words. See if there is any difference.

4 Go into a toyshop or a toy department and study the displays. Pick out toys which by the pictures on them or the way they are displayed indicate that they are for girls and see what they suggest girls should do or be. Do the same for boys' toys.

5 See how often a father-son relationship pictured on a toy or in an advertisement will be an outdoor, creative one, and how often a mother-daughter relationship will be connected with the house in some way. (Yet mothers often in real life bowl cricket balls to their sons or play tennis with their daughters.)

6 Observe and list soap advertisements which result in little girls looking pretty, feminine, soft. Note those where boys' clothes are dirty from sport or where boys are resisting being washed, 'like a real boy'.

3 EQUALITY OF EDUCATION

In theory boys and girls receive equal education. They often go to the same schools. They sit for the same examinations. They are often taught by the same teachers. The law which says that education is compulsory applies to girls just as much as boys. Teachers receive the same training. In theory, then, there would appear to be a great deal of equality in education. In fact, this is not so.

When the child leaves the shelter of his or her home and starts school, the subtle conditioning or sex role education, already described in Chapter 2, not only continues, but grows in strength and influence. To this are added more positive discriminations.

The conditioning and sex role education starts with school readers, from which boys and girls learn their first words. In these books mums are mostly pictured in aprons and in the kitchen or waving dads off to work. Women are seen in passive and supporting roles, such as housewife, nurse, secretary. Fathers are shown doing interesting, meaningful jobs. Boys take the lead in action and adventures, they help to rescue little girls or animals, and generally act in a creative, managing, responsible manner. Girls are pictured in passive, supporting, quiet roles, following the boys, helping them in their creative actions. They are happy, gay, pretty, efficient, but they rarely take the lead. If you think this is an exaggeration, go and have a look at some of the readers used in primary classes in school. Read the picture books of younger members of a family. I, myself, am the author of over twenty books for children, ranging from the first books to junior novels. In my early books, which were adventure type stories, I always put the boy in the leading dominating role. I did not do this deliberately. It just seemed the right thing to do. I am sure now I was influenced by all the similar books I had read.

But when I came to write books from real life, historical stories, I found that girls took the lead. This is because, long before my knowledge of the theory of feminism or conditioning, I had become concerned with the historical injustices visited on girls, and so battling girls, one a suffragette, one a convict's daughter, became my heroines. Again, I did not do it consciously. It just reflected the way I was thinking.

In *The Gender Trap*, Carol Adams and Rae Laurikietis discuss the 'hidden messages' of nursery rhymes and fairy tales;

> 'lovely maidens and princesses usually have to wait passively for some prince to come along. All other females are ugly hags, witches or stepmothers (invariably wicked). None of the females

do anything worthwhile. Men do the rescuing and the brainwork, they are independent, brave and given to overcoming insurmountable difficulties. Women are rarely friends with each other, they compete. Women can rarely change their own lives — they have to wait for men to do it for them.'

In Glenys Lobban's article in *Forum for the Discussion of New Trends in Education,* she analyses the sex roles in reading schemes widely used in schools. The range of activities for boys included playing with cars, trains, football, lifting or pulling heavy objects, gardening, playing cricket. For girls it was preparing the tea, playing with dolls, taking care of brothers and sisters. The boys took the lead in active, adventurous activities, the girls only in domestic activities, skipping and hopping. The adult roles shown for girls included only family roles, mother, grandmother, aunt, while for boys they also included many jobs: fishermen, farmers, bus drivers, and others.

Now you may say that the roles that are shown in these books and stories merely reflect what happens in real life, and you would be quite right. It is a vicious circle. Women are shown in these roles, so they adopt these roles. One does not deny this fact, but it does not mean that all women *want* to fill these roles. It is what society allots them. Also it is very good if girls — and boys — realise that their books are reflecting stereotyped sex roles, which they, the readers, are therefore influenced by to carry on in their own lives. It is good if they realise these roles are not necessarily the best or the only roles open to them. Their books echo what they are and the majority echo their books.

So if a boy or a girl wants to be something different, or finds he or she is different, and this makes them feel odd, they can take strength from knowing that the books reflect what is happening and what has been happening for a long time, but that there is absolutely no good reason why it should continue, why present-day children should follow those roles if they do not want to. It is also good if they know that there are many other boys and girls who, like themselves, feel odd in the roles allotted to them and would prefer to be different.

Unfortunately this conditioning imposed on girls in pre-school and early school life not only greatly colours the view they have of themselves and their future role in life but it also influences their attitude towards their education and their achievement in education, and this is a much more serious matter. A woman can, in later life, look back on the conditioning to which she was subjected, and she can overcome it to some extent, but if it has resulted in her not making the full use of her educational opportunities, she usually finds herself in a position where she cannot alter her situation.

Because she has so often wasted her school days, or left school too early, she finds herself without useful qualifications and in the least rewarding and most underpaid jobs. She will either be at a great economic disadvantage in the workforce or completely economically dependent on her husband. This inferiority or dependence then results in her becoming even more inferior and dependent. She begins to lose what expertise, knowledge or confidence she had.

The whole basis of the problem is that because girls are expected to get married and become wives and mothers, they and their parents tend to take less interest in their education. As a result, they do become wives and mothers. It is another vicious circle. This is probably the greatest inequality in the educational system, and it is a very subtle one. A girl's education is not considered as important as a boy's. Because it is taken for granted she will get married, parents do not take the same trouble over what subjects a girl studies, what she qualifies for, indeed whether she qualifies at all.

There are many statistics to prove that girls leave school earlier than boys. Parents will go to tremendous lengths to keep a boy at school, to encourage him to study, to insist he does an apprenticeship or goes on to further education. The choice of a job or a career is considered one of the most important things in a boy's life. In most homes it is discussed at great length, and he is offered as wide a choice as his family's economic situation allows.

With a girl, however, parents do not think it important whether she studies or not, they generally do not take the same interest in what she does, and they generally are not prepared to spend the same money on her education. Once again, if you do not believe me, start listening to how people talk about their children's education, and hear how, in contrast to the way they discuss a son's education, they will say something like: 'Of course, it doesn't matter about Mary. She's sure to get married', or 'Betty's not much of a student. But that does not matter, of course.'

My own life was a perfect example of this. My mother went to the greatest lengths to make my brother study. She heard his work. She badgered him to keep at his books. She waited on him hand and foot. He did two years 'matriculation', as it was called then, and my mother made great sacrifices for him to go to a university college.

In my own case, I was constantly being told not to study any more. 'You've done enough for tonight.' 'You'll get too tired.' 'Come and make a four for us.' My parents were avid bridge players, and as a result of this I never achieved the educational standard of which I was capable, but, at the age of nine, I became quite a good bridge player! My parents, of course, were as much a product of the system as I was. They firstly believed that the role of a woman was to get married. I had a particularly happy and secure childhood, and could not have had kinder parents. Just as my mother made great sacrifices to send my brother to the university, so did she make great sacrifices to send me to a private school. She did this because she thought going to a private school would make me more socially acceptable and able to make a better marriage.

My father was also wonderfully good to me, and made me the independent person I am. At a very early age he took me to cricket and football matches. I saw Bradman make his famous century against Larwood, and I have always been a great sports follower and participant. My father and I were the greatest of friends. We frequently went on hikes together, into the country and down to the beach. At a very early age I went into his small publishing business, and worked with him. He taught me many practical things and at every stage in life encouraged my independence and abilities.

For all this, I recognised myself in Germaine Greer's book as the product of many of the disabilities under which girls suffer. Thus, at the age of only fifteen, when I said I wanted to leave school, no one tried to prevent me. I had always said I would do two years in the sixth form and then go to university, and my parents had not discouraged me. Then, at that all-important and restless age of fifteen, when I suddenly discovered boys and began to be interested in new clothes and in going out, for just one brief period of a few months I thought it would be fun to leave school, start work, and earn some money of my own. What a familiar story! I hear it from girls all the time.

My parents encouraged this too. They obviously could not see

19

any great advantage in my staying at school, and they were having a struggle keeping my brother at the university. Had I been a boy any thought of my leaving school would have been discouraged immediately. I would have been told I must make a career for myself. I must get better qualifications. And I would have been easily persuaded. Within a year I realised I had made a terrible mistake, and I then started a part-time university course, which meant I could not do honours. The result was I ended up with the most useless university qualification anyone can have, a pass arts degree.

This sort of thing is continually happening to girls. During their whole school career their parents and friends expect less of them. They do not expect them to plan for a great career. Education is something to make them a more sociably acceptable person, and a career or job is something they pursue between leaving school and getting married.

Following this same principle, girls are encouraged to do 'suitable' subjects at school, socially acceptable subjects. It goes back to the time when girls did not go to school at all, but stayed at home and learnt the social graces — reading, writing, painting, sewing, playing the piano, even, if they were wealthy, travelling abroad and learning languages. Thus, at school, girls are encouraged to do the ladylike, suitable subjects like English, history and languages, but not the sciences or mathematics which are considered more difficult and more manly subjects. In my own case I came top in algebra and geometry (as they were then called) in my intermediate year, but no one, including myself, gave the slightest thought to the idea that I would go on with mathematics, even though I enjoyed it. If I were going to do anything of note, my parents always said, I was 'going to write', a socially acceptable occupation for a woman (think of Jane Austen!). My brother did a science course, and yet his school results were never as good as mine.

Study the final exam results every year, and see how many more girls do English literature than maths or sciences, and see how well girls now do in both areas. They dominate the humanities. And what is the result? Girls end up with a lot of qualifications that are too often useless (except for teaching) when it comes to following a career or seeking a job. Teaching, of course, is another of those areas considered 'suitable' for women, as it deals with caring for the young. On the whole, if girls stay at school, they are 'educated' rather than trained for a career.

There is, of course, nothing wrong in being 'educated'. It is a great pity that everyone is not properly educated in literature, art and philosophy. One of the faults of our present educational system is that people who become lawyers, doctors, politicians, etc. are often good in their professions but are not properly educated. As it is now, the men tend to follow those careers which give them the greatest economic return and the greatest decision-making power, without being educated in the widest way, while women end up with an education and without economic and decision-making power, doing menial, repetitive work.

This results in men, with the decision-making power, often lacking the resources to make the right decisions, and women being discontented because their abilities are not being properly used. Then they lose even those abilities.

Another subtle obstruction that is often put in a girl's way is perhaps the most discouraging of all. That is the impression, by direct statement or by implication, that it does not do for a girl to be too clever. 'The boys won't like you if you're too clever'. Because boys are brought up to be the leader or dominating person in a male-female relationship, they prefer a girl who is not as clever as they are. All these things combine to prevent a girl getting the best qualifications or using her abilities to her greatest benefit.

The disadvantages and difficulties mentioned so far are ones of influence and attitudes, and they are probably the most important. But there are also definite positive physical and material inequalities in the system under which girls suffer.

One is in the actual facilities made available to them. In mixed state schools, there are sometimes separate playgrounds for boys and girls, and the area for girls is often less than that for boys. This is justified by the statement that boys are rougher, noisier and more active than girls and therefore need more space. But we have already seen that girls are often only less active and noisy because they are made to behave like this, and the smaller or less adequate playing facilities will reinforce this.

The same applies to single sex schools. The playing area in the girls' school are often smaller and far inferior to those in boys' schools. The variety of sports offered girls in their schools is also smaller. In mixed schools there is every now and then a story reported of a girl who wants to play football or rugger, and is not allowed to. Those sports are for boys. In some schools there are separate gymnasia. Girls dance and do 'keep fit' exercises in theirs, while boys play volley ball or something equally strenuous in theirs. Often there are no mixed teams, and there are separate instructors and tuition.

In class work it is the same. In *The Gender Trap*, the authors talk about the ways in which schools keep alive the idea that men and women are different, by offering girls and boys different facilities and choices. Even in primary schools, teachers often expect different styles of work from boys and girls. Girls are assumed to want to make things look nice, boys to know how they work. Most girls' schools have poorer science facilities than do boys'. Girls at mixed schools usually have better access to science equipment, and though the gap in achievement in science between boys and girls widens as they move through the school, this gap is not so wide where facilities are there for both.

As far as practical subjects are concerned, girls are still encouraged to do needlework and home economics in many schools. Boys take metalwork, woodwork, technical drawing, subjects girls may not even be allowed to take. Equally, boys may not be encouraged or allowed to do typing or domestic science.

In secondary schools girls still do mainly arts subjects, and are encouraged towards 'female' studies and careers that are 'suitable'. This usually means careers that fit in with marriage and having children. If we set out to tell girls and boys that there are 'women's jobs' and 'men's jobs', we couldn't have thought of a better way of doing it!

Even over school outings, girls and boys may be treated differently. Girls may visit the local nursery, while boys go round the steelworks. Punishments differ — boys are caned more often, and generally treated more roughly. In assembly, girls may sit while boys stand, presumably training for their future role as protectors or the weaker sex.

Virginia Woolf recognised certain other discriminations against women in the education system in her essay, *A Room of One's Own*, written in 1929, in which she sought the solution to the obvious inequality in the achievement of the sexes. Her thoughts on the subject started after she had 'lunched off partridge' in a men's college and 'dined on prunes and custard' in a women's dormitory. She only half reached the solution, blaming the situation on such things as physical disabilities, economic dependence, lack of encouragement, and the lack of 'a room of one's own'. Why then after over forty years, when most of these things have been overcome, are women still in inferior positions? It took more years before women began to analyse and recognise the severe conditioning against achievement under which they were reared. Simone de Beauvoir wrote at length about it in *The Second Sex,* a book that is still a classic on the subject.

So far we have discussed conditioning mainly as it affects girls, but the same conditioning also applies to boys, and whereas girls suffer in their educational achievement through not enough pressure being put on them, boys probably suffer through too much. They are constantly being exhorted to do well at work, to study, to follow a career, to be successful, to be a leader, to make money.

This is fine for a boy who is born with leadership qualities or who is naturally ambitious. Some people feel a great driving need to achieve, proved by those who reach great heights in spite of innumerable obstacles, such as a poor economic background or physical handicaps. So this type of boy, given every encouragement, will thrive and no doubt be a great success in material terms.

But what of the boy who has no great ability or no great natural drive? What of the boy who does not want to be a great leader or make a lot of money? He too is given little option by society. He must strive and work hard, possibly go to war, or take on responsibilities he would rather avoid.

There must be many a man who has achieved very little, and looks back on a miserable life of striving, battling, studying, working hard in some uncongenial occupation, for example as a clerk, when he would perhaps have much preferred an outdoor, practical job or a so-called 'feminine' job, such as nursing or kindergarten teaching, without great potential for advancement or leadership. So boys too suffer from conditioning, and when feminists say they want to free women from their conditioning, they also say they want to free men. They believe that in freeing women they will free men.

It must be said again, however, that, although men do also suffer from conditioning, their conditioning results in their having the educational, economic and political power, so the women suffer the most. They end up having none of these.

Which brings us back to one final point about girls and their education. All the subtle and blatant disadvantages which they suffer, and which have been discussed in this chapter, are based on the one big assumption that education is not as important for girls as it is for boys, and the very strange thing about this assumption is that it is totally wrong.

In fact, it is far *more* important for girls, or women, to have a good education and good qualifications than for men, because a girl, to achieve the same rewards, will always have to be much better than a man. Firstly, if she does not get married, she will get nowhere without qualifications. Secondly, if she gets married and is forced or wants to work, she will have to overcome so many additional handicaps and such an additional work load that once again she needs the best qualifications she is capable of obtaining.

Let us look at the first proposition. If a girl does not get married, she will always have to prove herself a better person in any field of work. There is a long-established attitude among those who make the appointments that women are inferior to men, and a girl has to work very hard and be very efficient to persuade decision-makers otherwise. Again this is slowly changing. But at present most decisions about appointments and advancement are made by older men, and it is practically impossible to change the attitude of such men.

Also, there is always an opportunity for a boy with absolutely no qualifications to get on in the world. A girl without any qualifications will find it very hard to get any job beyond that paying the lowest rates, without any hope of promotion and often doing menial or boring work. This means that such girls often marry young and for the wrong reasons. Marriage offers them a hope of something better. So the girl who is not particularly academic should make sure she stays at school as long as possible and has some qualifications after school to fit her for positions such as a typist, nurse, policewoman, hairdresser, etc. The academic girl should make sure she gets as good academic qualifications as possible.

There are three types of married women who work. There are those who are forced to, because they are the sole breadwinners for their children, or because their husbands do not or cannot earn enough to keep them and their families. Work for these women is sheer drudgery, for at the end of their working day they come home to another full work load. The need for such a woman to be able to earn as much as possible in as satisfactory a job as possible is obvious.

Then there is the woman who wants to keep working at her career, while and in between having her family. She will lose both time and expertise while bearing her children, and will also have prejudices to fight in the employment field, so she too needs particularly good qualifications.

Finally, there is the largest number of working wives, who decide to look after their children themselves when the children are little, but then wish to return to the workforce, either to add to the family finances or for self-fulfilment. The number of women in this category is rapidly growing. Families are smaller and women are living longer. After about six to ten years of childbearing and rearing, the majority of women now find their children no longer need them to the same extent and do not take up as much time.

If this type of woman has qualifications she will have lost several years of knowledge and experience, so the better her qualifications the more likely she is to obtain a good job. And what happens to her if she has allowed herself to leave school too early or has no qualifications? The only jobs available are the lowest paid, least satisfactory, most boring. They tend to be similar to those she is already doing in the home — working in food or clothing factories, office cleaning, as tea ladies etc.

These jobs suit some people, and that is fine. If women are happy continuing to work in the home, or working in domestic type jobs, there is nothing wrong in that. The main thing is that people should be allowed to do what they like. If a woman wants a different sort of job, then it is tragic if that woman finds herself at the age of thirty-five or forty, with her most useful child-rearing days finished, with many years of health and strength ahead of her, and with absolutely no qualifications whatsoever. My generation is littered with women of this sort, who regret bitterly that they did not finish the courses they gave up to get married.

SUGGESTIONS FOR OBSERVATION AND DISCUSSION

1 With a co-educational school, see if you can find any areas of discrimination against girls, such as sports they are not allowed to pursue, smaller sporting areas, smaller study areas, positions of authority among students from which they are barred.

2 With a single-sex school, study a similar school of the other sex. See if you can find discriminatory areas in the girls' school, such as fewer or smaller sports fields, fewer sports available to them, subjects or courses they are not able to follow, inferior teaching, smaller science laboratories, subjects or courses they are particularly encouraged to do which will lead them into 'feminine' and lower-paid occupations. Compare the extra curricular activities in boys' and girls' schools such as hikes, trips, scouts, etc.

3 With a co-educational school, see if there are (a) any subjects such as woodwork that a girl is not allowed to do, or not encouraged to do, or (b) any subjects such as domestic science, typing or dressmaking that boys are not allowed to do, or are discouraged from doing either by staff or other students, such as a boy being laughed at or called a 'sissy'. Discuss this honestly. Find out if there are boys who would like to do typing or cooking if encouraged, or girls who would like to do woodwork.

4 See if there are any career books or career guides or career counselling in school libraries or schools. See if there is any difference between the types of careers that are suggested for boys or girls, either by word or by the illustrations used.

5 Bring up casually in a conversation with a group of adults the question of whether education is more important for girls or boys. At some stage ask what would happen if there was only enough money to keep either a son or a daughter at school, or send a son or a daughter to university or to an advanced college of education.

6 Bring up casually in conversation with adults whether they think a girl should be a plumber or a carpenter or a bricklayer or a boy should be a nurse or a typist. If they say no, ask their reasons. Discuss the reasons given. Among the answers will probably be that the first listed jobs are not 'suitable' for girls, and the second listed jobs will not bring 'advancement' to boys. Think and discuss honestly the position into which this puts girls. If manual tasks are not suitable for girls, why are they suited to scrubbing floors, washing nappies, waiting on the family at dinner? If nursing and typing do not offer good career opportunities for boys why are so many girls encouraged to undertake them? Why are the less good options good enough for girls?

4 THE CONFLICT OF CONFORMING

In spite of the many inequalities in a girl's education, subtle and not so subtle, there are always many girls who continue to do well. Figures show that up to about the age of twelve girls at school tend to do better than boys. Obstacles are meant to be overcome, and people with ability often achieve more when they face handicaps or disabilities, either economic or physical. Also, many a father, no matter how much he believes in girls being 'feminine' or in marriage for girls, cannot help being proud of a daughter excelling at sport or at work at school, and if he is intelligent or well educated will often help her with her studies.

There will also always be girls born with stronger wills, or more aggressive traits in their characters, who will resist their early conditioning. To quote Germaine Greer:

> The growing girl may refuse to keep her room neat, may insist on mucking about with boyish affairs, even to the extent of joining a male group and fighting to maintain her place in it by being twice as tough as any of the boys. She may lose all her hankies and hair-ribbons, rip her knickers climbing trees, and swear and swagger with the best of them. This is patronizingly referred to as going through a difficult phase, but we may find evidence of the duration of this kind of resistance over years and years, *until pubery delivers the final crushing blow.*

The italics are mine. It is at that terrible time of puberty, when boys and girls first find their bodies developing in strange ways, when they first experience sexual urges, when they first become conciously aware of their sex differences and first become sexually aware of the other sex; it is at that very difficult time that girls first become actively conscious of the fact that they are not only different from boys, but that they must also be different from their true selves. They must all conform to one predestined, laid down pattern. It is when they first learn to dissemble, to be deceitful. It is the time when girls find that it is no longer enough to be good at something they like, they must be good at appealing to boys.

The whole of society and the world of power, the press, the media, advertising, magazines, stories, books, comics, all the great pressures that business, society, parents, peers and other people can wield, all these pressures are brought to bear on a girl to make her conform to society's view of what a girl should be. Not for her the choice between being a doctor, a lawyer, a plumber or an artist. For her is only the choice between being attractive, a socially successful person or a failure, between becoming what women are expected to be, a wife and a mother, or being considered peculiar, unsatisfied, unfulfilled.

To quote Greer again:

We are constantly aware that puberty is hell. It is hell for boys as well as girls, but for boys it is a matter of adjusting to physical changes which signify the presence of sex and genitality, as well as to the frustration of genital urges. For the girl it is a different matter: she has to arrive at the feminine posture of passivity and sexlessness.

The girl not only has to adjust to her physical changes, she has to change her whole character. She could overcome her physical problems, if she did not also have to face the tremendous confusion of changing her personality, of hiding any natural abilities she may have, of becoming the perfect little, doll-like person that boys and parents either like or are brought up to think they like. 'If', says Greer, 'she cannot strike an equilibrium between her desires and her conditioning this is when she breaks down, runs away, goes wrong, begins to fail in school, to adopt forms of behaviour which are not only anti-social but self-destructive.'

Germaine Greer tends to use strong words that antagonise people. When she says 'self-destructive' she does not mean anything physically violent, but that a girl destroys herself at this stage because, in her eagerness to conform, she loses her will to be herself, her urge to be creative, her wish to achieve, her very confidence in herself. Just at that time when a young person's future career is being decided, when what subjects he or she is to specialise in are being considered, when whether he or she is to leave school or not is being discussed, the average girl suddenly finds that her parents or her friends do not really want her to achieve. They want her to conform.

If she is to be a social success she must repress many of the things she wants to do. She now consciously learns she must act, dress, make up her face to attract boys, she must smile when she does not want to, she must appear less tomboyish, even less clever. What has been conditioning, unnoticed by the girl, now comes out in the open.

McCall's, an American magazine for women, which is typical of all magazines for women in that its emphasis in articles and stories is on the woman as the home-maker, the supporter and pleaser of man, published the following under the heading 'Pediatrician's Almanac' by Dr Lendon H Smith:

Mothers should teach their daughters to be clean, smart, attractive, friendly, and — most important — a little weaker and a little less knowledgeable (not less wise) than a male. I worry about any girl's becoming, for instance, a great athlete — especially a runner. She might run so fast she'd never get caught by a boy.

You think that is funny? It is not really. It is tragic and true.

Nor is this hiding of a girl's best abilities the end of her problems. The whole system of women's magazines, the press, radio and television, advertising and articles maintain a continuous barrage, telling her what is wrong with her. She has bad breath, she smells, her hair is dirty, too dry, or too greasy, she is too short or too tall, she is too fat or too thin, her face is pimply, her skin is too dry or too greasy. There's always something wrong with her.

The whole horrible monstrosity of cosmetics advertising is not only aimed at creating a need in a girl which is hardly ever there, so that it continually undermines her confidence in her natural self, but that need is nearly always allied with being a success with a boy or a man. As soon as she uses a certain toothpaste, or soap or perfume, or shampoo, her boy friend will like her again. 'How long is it since a man touched your hair?' asks a typical advertisement. Even if a girl takes a certain cough mixture and gets over a cold, she is a social success again, and the boys flock around her. (It makes one wonder about the 'in sickness and health' idea of love.) Pressure is put on a girl from all sides to attract the other sex.

The years when girls face their first dancing classes or dances or parties can be absolute agony for them, and in my opinion many girls never recover their confidence again. Up till then they have either achieved or not achieved happily enough in school. If they were good at work or sport they were given good marks, possibly prizes, or selected for teams. If they were not particularly good at anything, it was not a matter of great moment. No great pressures were put on them. After all, they were only girls, so lack of success at work or sport did not really mean they were great failures.

Suddenly they face dating and dances. They talk about nothing else. Their mothers spend hours buying or making them suitable dresses. Very few girls are ever the perfect beings they are expected to be, but at this age particularly they tend to be too fat or too thin or too tall or too short. Girls — and boys — develop very unevenly and at different ages. Mothers discuss whether this or that dress suits them, in front of the shop girls. A young girl immediately becomes conscious of her every physical disability.

Then come the parties or dances themselves. Girls are lined up, either actually or in more subtle ways, to be selected by boys. It is something like a cattle market. Suddenly some young girls find they are for some probably quite stupid reason, not acceptable to boys. Alternatively, a girl may find she does not particularly want to dance with any of the boys or to be the sort of person that boys or society want her to be.

But whether she wants to be that sort of person or not, she is quickly conscious of whether she is socially a success or a failure. She now consciously realises the terrible penalty for not being able to conform.

There is a most moving story by Henry Handel Richardson about a girl's first ball. There are the discussions among the adults beforehand, the instructions given to her about how to attract partners, how to smile. Then there is her failure. No one wants to dance with her. She goes home completely humiliated. She hears the adults discussing her failure. Finally there comes the realisation that she has not only failed, but she has betrayed herself. *She* did not want to dance with the boys any more than they wanted to dance with her. She had sat there all night with a fixed, idiotic smile on her face, trying for something she did not even want.

Demands to conform start early in a girl's life, and go on through adolescence and adulthood. It has always been difficult for girls and women to do things which are not thought 'womanly'. Consider some of the great women novelists of the last century, the Bronte sisters, who all had to give men's names when presenting their work to publishers. So did George Eliot, whose real name was Mary Ann Evans. These women understood through their own experience what it was like for a woman to try and break into a 'man's world'. And despite being successful themselves, they had great understanding of the agonies of 'failure', and the problems faced by women having to conform to society's image of them.

In *The Obstacle Race,* Germaine Greer describes the barriers and frustrations that for so long blocked the way to acceptance of women painters as artists in their own right — both by the male world and themselves. For in the world of art too, traditional ideas of how a woman should live have often robbed women of the chance of excellence and condemned many women artists to oblivion — either by neglect or through their work being credited to someone else. Her arguments for why there are no female Leonardos or Titians are not that women have babies, or smaller brains or lack energy, but that their energies have often been diverted into distracting or unsatisfactory channels, and their sense of themselves too often damaged.

I can hear you raising all sorts of objections here, saying that boys also go through agonies at this stage. Boys who are short or fat or pimply are rejected by girls. They are lonely. They cannot get the girls they want. This is all true. But at least boys *have a choice.* They can go and ask a girl for a dance or a date, and a girl will often agree. If she does not, a boy can retire. Have you noticed how few boys will dance with an unattractive or unacceptable girl? They would rather stand and talk with the other boys, and no one condemns them for that. They are not considered a social failure. If anything, it adds to their attraction. Also, if they have no dates, they can get on with other things such as their careers or their sport.

But the girl who is left sitting at a dance is a failure. Everyone notices it. She does not have a choice even to ask the boy that attracts her. To gain his attention, she has to preen and primp, cover her face with make-up, wear modish clothes, often uncomfortable (too tight or too cold or too hot), often outrageous, she has to curl or colour her hair, she giggles and carries on, often talks too loudly. In effect, she goes through a whole succession of stupidities just to attract attention. The whole business not only takes up a great deal of time and money, but distracts her from more important and creative thoughts and ideas.

As a young girl there were times when I would have dearly loved to ask certain boys for a dance or for a date, but such was not my right. Such was my fear of being a 'wallflower' at a dance that I often danced with boys I disliked or went out with boys of no great appeal. What is even worse, some girls get married to boys they think they 'love', but do not greatly like, simply because they feel they must get married. Also, in today's more permissive society girls often sleep with boys they do not particularly like.

Magazines sometimes give a veneer of being liberated but are no different in their basic assumptions about women from the more conservative ones, and often influence girls towards this sort of acquiescence.

In today's more liberal social climate, it is probably preferable that young people, planning marriage, sleep or even live together first. This reveals whether they are compatible, both sexually and in their personalities, and probably avoids many unhappy marriages. But it is very sad when a young girl feels she must sleep with boys to prove her popularity, or to show that she is 'not a square'. This is not only an invasion of her privacy and her freedom of choice, but can often result in her becoming pregnant, thus damaging the whole course of her life.

What an agonising conflict it all is for a young girl. On one side there is the wish to be herself. On the other are all the pressures to do or be something different. The young girl has already been trained, unconsciously, to be passive, supportive, kind, loving, quiet, neat, conscientious, negative, so she is in no position to resist the pressures now teaching her that she must consciously conform to a certain pattern.

She must be very clever, and attract boys, without appearing to be clever. She is told her faults, and she must cover them up with make-up. She must repress many of her natural urges and natural abilities, because these turn boys off.

Is it any wonder, with this terrible conflict, this terrible denial of a girl's true nature and natural self, that she loses her creativity, her originality, her true personality, her confidence in herself? She takes refuge in all those silly things that make one feel ashamed of one's sex. She starts to giggle. A giggle is often a way of covering up a girl's wish to say something, or to make a point in an argument or conversation, in a 'feminine', non-aggressive way. Alternatively it is used to cover up her growing lack of confidence in herself or her abilities.

Because of her anxiety to please, she is constantly distracted from what she wants to do or what she is doing. When she opens her mouth to speak she is always aware of the effect she is making, growing more and more nervous about expressing a point of view, fearing she will be ridiculed. She becomes increasingly nervous about speaking in public, fearing she will either appear too clever or look foolish.

What happens then? These conflicting feelings become pent up inside her so she becomes emotional, temperamental, bursts into tears easily. In many cases the strain is so great that she gives up trying to be herself or to achieve anything creative; she ceases doing well at school, and concentrates fully on the boy-catching race. She then begins to grow catty about other girls, fearing their competition, so we hear the oft-reported view that women will not support women.

She wastes endless time and money on plastering her face with unnatural make-up. Has anyone noticed the ridiculous amount of make-up many young girls wear? The reason some feminists are worried by make-up is that it detracts from a girl's natural, healthy looks, and also it makes all girls look alike, all painted to the fashionable pattern.

This concentration on appearance and the effect she is making means the growing girl reads women's magazines instead of newspapers. She does not know what is going on, for who is interested in her views on politics? And thus, of course, she knows less and less about politics or current affairs, so it is another vicious circle. Her knowledge and views on these matters decrease and she does become less worth listening to. Then her lack of confidence is increased. The magazines, in their turn, reinforce all the homemaking, self-adorning, man-pleasing qualities a girl is supposed to have. Their articles and advertisements are almost exclusively on these subjects.

In sport it is the same. A girl is taught she must not look too determined or intense (has anyone told a boy that?), or perhaps it is implied by someone poking fun at her. 'Hey, you looked funny when you hit that ball — so fierce.' So what happens? She starts to hit the tennis ball with a giggle or a smile. By concentrating on her appearance she ceases to concentrate on the ball.

With many girls, they become so self-conscious about their appearance at sport, and they do so increasingly badly at it, that they give up sport altogether. It is yet another vicious circle. Because they give up sport, they do become worse at it, and they have more time to spend on clothes and make-up, on talking about boys and dating. As a result, boys become the most important things in their life. Boys talk about girls also, of course, but it is usually only as a part of a normally busy life.

Here, I was lucky, and escaped the worst of these pressures. I was brought up very strictly in a Methodist Church and home. Although the teaching was strict, we had lots of fun. We had tennis at the church courts, we went for hikes and picnics, we had an active Girl Guide movement, and we had good discussion groups. My father took me to watch a great deal of sport. So, although I left school early because of my interest in clothes and boys, I was fortunate that my many other activities taught me to be independent and active, so boys were far from my only concern. Also, I was not allowed to wear make-up, which certainly did me no harm.

It was my family and Methodist upbringing, and also our lack of money, that saved me from another pressure to which girls are subject. That is the pressure of dress. A girl becomes a slave to fashion. Of course, this also happens to boys. They too follow fashions, but for some strange reason boys' fashions are never actually uncomfortable. Girls' fashions are often quite ridiculous, featuring such things as high heels, clogs, short dresses, long dresses, tight dresses, fine stockings. Over and over again I have seen girls completely hindered in their activities through the clothes they wear. And once again one can only blame this on the media, the consumer society, and on the pressure on girls to be socially acceptable.

After all, if a boy is short, that's bad luck and he may not be as popular with the girls as a tall boy, but the pressure to succeed with the opposite sex is not so great on him that he will cripple himself wearing five-inch heels or clogs to make himself look taller.

Have you ever wondered why so many girls fainted in nineteenth century novels? It was not only because it was considered feminine and attracted attention (which it did); it was mainly because their frocks and corsets were drawn so tightly to give them tiny waists.

Everyone by now must know that women's liberation is continually allied with 'burning bras'. The first thing to say is that this event never even happened! But it is still possible to see what it could mean as a symbolic demonstration against many things, but mainly against the artificiality and deception that society enforces on women in both their way of life and their clothes.

At one time, bras had become monstrous things. It was impossible to buy a bra that was comfortable. If you were large in the bust, they were wired, shaped and too tight, if you were small in the bust, they were wired and padded. One could not buy a simple, comfortable garment that gave support, if support were wanted. In other words, all women at that time, as at all times, were being made to conform to the fashionable shape of that particular phase, and all had identical, pushed-up, padded-out breasts.

Why should a woman be judged by the size and shape of her breasts? Why should a woman wear clothes that are uncomfortable just because they are fashionable? Why should a woman wear a bra at all if she does not want to? Why must a woman be so self-conscious if she is not perfect? In other words, why cannot women be their natural selves in shape, size and colouring, without excessive fashion or cosmetics. Which does not say, of course, that all girls or women should go braless. If a girl wants to wear one, or feels her figure needs one, then she should wear one. But for goodness sake let her stop being so self-conscious about her shape and size.

The more I know of conditioned women (and that includes myself), the more I despair of their need to conform to the given pattern. Thoroughly pleasant-looking girls who are a little plump are always dieting to be thin. Thin girls want to be fat. Short girls are conscious of their shortness and want to be tall. Tall girls want to be short. All that is necessary is a healthy and clean body, clean, shining hair and lots of exercise. A plain face is only plain until one becomes familiar with its expressions and the character behind it. There is nothing more destructive of a girl's character, good looks and confidence in herself than for her to take up too much time with her clothes and her make-up.

SUGGESTIONS FOR OBSERVATION AND DISCUSSION

1 See how many advertisements in the press, magazines, radio and TV you can find which show that a girl is lacking or in need of some article to improve herself. How many similar advertisements can you find featuring boys or men?

2 See how many advertisements you can find in which the weakness or need in girls is allied with attracting boys or men.

3 Study women's magazines, from the most sophisticated to the most simple, and see how their articles and advertisements connect girls and women with home-making activities, cooking, sewing, knitting, doing things to please boys or men. See how few times there is an article about girls and careers outside the home. See how often trendy women's magazines which do discuss careers for married women also give hints on how to fit these in with household chores, or how not to upset their husbands.

4 Have a discussion among boys and girls or young people. Ask the boys to say honestly if a girl who is too clever or beats them at sport appeals to them. Ask the girls if they have ever felt they have committed a social mistake by being too clever or too good at sport.

5 In the same sort of group discuss cosmetic advertising in magazines,

and the use of cosmetics. Ask the boys if they really like heavy cosmetics on girls. Ask the girls how much money and time they spend on cosmetics. How many jars or tubes are in their pockets, handbags, school bags or on their dressing table at home? Do they feel it makes them more attractive? Who are they mainly trying to attract?

6 Ask boys whether they ever wear uncomfortable clothes. Ask girls whether they do. If so, why? Do they hinder their actions: walking, running, etc?

5 THE MIRAGE OF MARRIAGE

I wish to state quite clearly that I have nothing in particular against marriage. There are happy marriages where both husband and wife enjoy doing things together, and both manage to lead good and full lives.

In an ideal society I believe marriage should be unnecessary, because if a man and women get the right sort of happiness and pleasure out of living together and bringing up their children together they would continue to do so without any legal enforcement. In our present stage of development, however, marriage is probably the best way for a man and a woman to live happily together, and it is certainly the best way to bring up children, although the present rate of marriage breakdown shows it is far from perfect. Some sort of family unit, though probably different from the present one, will always be necessary to offer children the love and security that is needed for them to become full and good people.

I also believe very strongly, however, that marriage as it operates at present is the greatest confidence trick that man has ever played on woman.

In getting married, under present conditions, the majority of women completely lose their independence, and this ultimately usually leads to their also losing their confidence, their self-respect, and even their capabilities.

It is a confidence trick because women do this willingly and happily, having been brought up to believe it is for their greatest good. When they get married, they believe they are getting everything they want and that they will live happily ever after. The truth is that although a women is kept, the average woman gets very little for herself. Man, on the other hand, gets the decision-making power because his wife is economically dependent on him, and he also, apart from his wife's keep, gets free sex, free housekeeping, and a free nurse to look after his children. In fact, he gains and continues to use the services of someone who will back him up, adjust to his way of life, support him, be there whenever he wants her at home, and will stay there when he wants to go out.

On top of all this he has managed to convey the impression that he is the 'caught' one. Countless jokes and remarks are made about men being caught, giving up their independence, losing their freedom, etc. People express mock-sorrow for the man getting married. Yet it is the woman for whom one should feel sorry, for she is sacrificing so much, but it takes her a long time to realise this.

The main trouble is that most girls marry for the wrong reasons and with the wrong expectations. Girls are brought up to be married. They are taught from birth as has already been indicated, that their role and main aim in life, their main objective, that for which they are best suited, that which will give them the greatest satisfaction and the greatest happiness, is marriage and motherhood. They grow up thinking it will be their life's main task and a life-long task.

During their entire girlhood, love and marriage are held up as glittering, worthwhile achievements. No matter how many marriages they know which have failed, or even if their parents are constantly at odds, they believe their marriage will be different.

As Byron says:

Man's love is a man's life a thing apart,
'Tis woman's whole existence.

Differently from women, marriage (and love and sex) for a man is only a part of his life. When he leaves the home, he gets on with the

main business of his life, which is making a career for himself, or building up his business. One of those kind and reassuring statements that are made to keep women happy in the service of men is that 'behind every great man stands a great woman'. And this is certainly true. There is a rueful remark made by businesswomen in high positions to each other: 'What I need is a good wife'. And a good wife is undoubtedly one of the greatest assets a man can have. If, however, he happens to have made a bad choice, and has a rotten, inefficient, dissatisfied or rebellious wife, he can still make his way quite well. He still has his work as a refuge. In many cases he will do even better at his job because it then becomes his whole life.

But a woman with a bad, inefficient, unco-operative, drunken or brutal husband has no redress at all. If she has children, which is usually the case, she will put them before her own interests, she will continue in a miserable position, housebound, short of money, and very unhappy. Unless she is a person of considerable mental resources, or with good work qualifications, she has no outlet for her unhappiness, no alternative way of life.

I have noticed when a famous man is interviewed on television and is asked what was the greatest day of his life (one of those questions loved by interviewers), he will pick out some high point in his career, artistic, political, sporting, or business. No matter how good a wife he has, he will not say his wedding day. The average woman, if asked the same question, will almost invariably say her wedding day or some day associated with her children or her husband. Her life seldom centres around her own achievements. She is always a supporter of sharer in, an appendage to, someone else's achievements.

Although after many years of domestic work I became a career woman, and although through all my years as a housewife I had some achievements in my own right, I must honestly say that the happiest day of my life was when I gave birth to my first child, a son. My joy, my positive exultation, was inexpressible, and I shall never forget it. It was not only because I loved children, and loved that small piece of humanity, but such had been my conditioning that I felt I had fulfilled my greatest destiny in life: I had produced a son. I had been absolutely terrified it would be a girl. My relief and happiness on that day are never to be forgotten.

The happiest *years* of my life were those before I was married and during my part-time course at the university, where, although I had to work extremely hard, I had a sense of achievement, and tremendous fun, spoiled only by my mother's persistent efforts to make me settle for one of the boys with whom I went out, and get married.

My other happiest years have been the last ten, when, after a lifetime of being in a supportive, backing-up role as a messenger, junior girl, typist, sub-editor, wife, mother, assistant editor, I finally became managing director of the family business. Since then I have enjoyed one of the fullest, happiest lives for which I could ask.

One of the pieces of luck that sets me apart from the average is that the position was there. However, I could not possibly have been equal to that position if I had not had the qualifications and had not served many years of apprenticeship in lowly positions in the company. Moreover, during all my domestic years, I kept my hand in and my brain alert by reading and writing, through the years of having babies, bathing them, feeding them and washing for them, driving them to and from school, helping them with their homework, etc. (I won't bore you with the endless chores).

Just as these have been the best years of my life, the *worst* years were those following the birth of my fourth child, when I had four children aged seven and under, when the aforesaid chores continued unremittingly from five in the morning until ten at night, when, for the only time in my life, I could not keep up my writing, and when I sometimes felt I could not go on. Yet I had many advantages, such as labour-saving devices, someone to help with the cleaning one morning a week, a husband on a good income so that we could afford the occasional baby-sitter and go out, good friends, a husband who was willing to help a little, and parents and friends who also helped a little. How much worse off are many women in similar positions?

And yet, on the other hand, I sometimes wonder if perhaps I was as badly off as any women with four children, for I hated, and grew to hate more and more all the work associated with homemaking. I would rather do a repetitive, clerical, writing or typing job any time than cook or look after children. I love children, but I hate all the work associated with them. Most women find housework dreary to some extent, but I really came to hate it. I hated it so much that I gradually built up my earnings through writing, until I needed to do less and less in the house.

All women are conditioned to marry and have children, and some women definitely enjoy the role. They are happy in the home, happy with the children, they enjoy cooking. There is a great tendency at present to condemn the women's movement for 'driving women out of the home', for 'making them feel guilty' when they do not want to take an *extra* job in addition to their work in the house.

This is absolutely untrue and shows how little people understand the real beliefs and aims of the women's movement. All they want to do is offer women a *choice*. In the past they have not had a proper choice. It was either marriage or a career and/or being an old maid, and both of the latter made women feel odd. If a woman married and worked outside the home it was usually because she had to supplement or provide the family income, which was sheer drudgery. It meant going to work, usually in a dreary job, during the day, and then coming home to the full complement of chores at night.

Married women hardly ever worked outside the home simply because they wanted to. If they did not have to work it was accepted that they would stay at home and look after the children, a full-time job, but for many a completely unsatisfying one. The rare woman who did work among my generation was the one who was made to feel guilty. She was neglecting her children. Friends of my daughters whose mothers worked were made to feel 'different', and to feel that their mothers were less than good.

Although I stayed at home for over twenty years to care for my children, I was even made to feel guilty because I wrote books, radio scripts, book reveiws, etc. I was often subjected to remarks implying that I was not satisfied with my life, that I was peculiar, that I was inadequate. Young people these days, when so many women work, will find this hard to believe, but it is true. The strange thing was that although I managed, by hard work, to make a few hours during the week available for writing, I was always there when the children came home from school, and always (until my fourth child) went to all the school open days, etc. And I noticed that many women who were considered 'all right' would be missing on these occasions for luncheons and cocktail parties. In other words, it was acceptable in the eyes of society for women to take time off for social affairs but not for serious, intellectual activities.

So, to repeat it again, all that feminists want to do is to offer a woman a choice. They have been deprived of a choice for so long that this is the basic premise of their thinking. The last thing they want to do is to apply pressure to work outside the home on the woman who is happy in the home. They believe many men would also be happier doing housework than the jobs they follow, and into which society has forced them. Today married people quite often change their roles, and many more men are sharing the household tasks, and working less hard at their careers. It makes their marriages happier.

However, feminists want to offer the woman who finds housework and child rearing repetitive, boring and dissatisfying, a choice too. They want to give her an opportunity to work at other things if she wants to, to achieve her full potential in other fields if this is what she wants.

They do not accept, and they fight at every point, the typical attitude and belief in our society that men and women are born basically different in their intellect or their aptitude. They accept that there are great differences in *people,* that some *people* do have a love and aptitude for child rearing, for manual tasks, for being supportive, but they think these differences lie within people of the same sex and not between one sex and another. They maintain that the apparent and obvious differences that can be seen all around us, between men and women, are the result of their conditioning and upbringing, of the pressures that society and the media bring to bear on them, not on their inherited character.

If women could take the same attitude as men that marriage is only a part of their life, instead of the whole of their life, feminists believe it would be better for women, for their children, for their husbands, and for society, for women would be happier, and women have a great deal to offer to the mainstream of society, not only one part of it.

I have spent some time on this subject, because it is one on which there are the greatest misunderstandings — misunderstandings that are constantly repeated in people's attitudes towards the women's movement.

Let us now have another look at how society does condition, influence and pressure women into getting married, sometimes with tragic, often with very unhappy results.

First of all there are the very early attitudes and pressures. We have seen how their toys, their early readers, their story books nearly all depict girls in mothering, wifely roles, making them think that is what they are meant for. When they grow older discussions and decisions about their education will be full of references to the fact that they will get married. Then, when they reach puberty, they learn that the most important thing for them is to appeal to boys. The extent of their success or failure at this all-important time will be measured by their looks, their ability to attract, to appeal to the other sex.

However, as I've already said, it is hard to keep a good girl down. There will always be those, and mercifully they are increasing in number, who resist their conditioning, whose parents are more enlightened, whose abilities are allowed to develop fully. They reach their twenties, they acquire qualifications or part-qualifications. Then they meet the final pressure from all sides.

'Has Mary got a steady boy friend?' asks the visiting aunt or friend.

'Aren't you married yet?' asks the jovial uncle or male visitor.

'Not married yet? You'll be on the shelf soon' says the happy man from next door.

'If you don't get married soon you'll be an old maid' says someone else's grandma.

'I wonder why she never married?' will be the inevitable remark by *someone* when an attractive unmarried woman around forty leaves the room.

And so it goes on. The pressure is always there. As with so many things these days, the situation is improving. Many girls with interesting or career jobs, their own businesses, and earning good money are sensible enough to realise what they would be giving up and they resist the pressure. They either stay unmarried or marry someone compatible, whom they really like, with whom they discuss such things as sharing the household chores, sharing the decision-making, etc. But for every girl who takes this attitude there are ten who marry too early, for the wrong reasons, and without any real understanding of the commitment they are undertaking.

Mothers are anxious to see their daughters married because they believe their daughters are a failure if they don't. They are also subject to pressure from other mothers whose daughters are married. Also they want to enjoy again the great day of their own marriage. For many a mother the second greatest event after her own marriage is her daughter's marriage. Families spend a ridiculously large amount of money on the actual ceremony of marriage, on the dresses, the receptions, the parties. This aspect is important because it often hides a hollow shell, often nothing more than a ceremony between two people, temporarily attracted to each other, or a great occasion for a girl, who is in love with the idea of love and marriage rather than with the person she is marrying.

Another thing that often forces girls into marriage is that because business people expect girls to marry, they do not employ them for responsible positions or do not promote them. Thus a girl is committed for her lifetime to a job in the already described supportive role. And because this is all her working career offers her, she does indeed get married. It is another of those vicious circles.

Advertising is another great force in making girls think marriage is important, and that if they get married they will live happily ever after. An advertisement for saving money, listing those things a man should save for, will almost invariably include his daughter's wedding. There are regular advertisements in the media for the trappings of marriage — engagement rings, wedding frocks, receptions, etc, — which stress the importance and glamour of the occasion. Advertisements for such things as washing powders, washing machines, tinned foods and refrigerators glamorise the role of housewife and mother. She is always looking clean, fresh, wearing a frilly apron, in a shining kitchen. All you need for clean clothes is to press a knob and use the right soap.

No one ever shows a housewife in shabby clothes, fed up, with an aching back or bedraggled hair, hanging out clothes on a freezing day with the wind whipping the wet clothes into her face. The sun is always shining when she hangs out the clothes. The refrigerators are always bursting with delicious food and drinks. No one ever shows the woman battling to make her money last a bit longer, or the woman with several hungry children, no money and a drunken or spendthrift husband. Advertisements for heating always show children with rounded limbs, clean shining hair, gurgling happily or laughingly playing. They are never shown dirty, grizzling, fighting, screaming, with running noses, refusing to be toilet trained.

It is in the interests of the decision-makers to make marriage appear glamorous and happy for women, so glamorous and happy it appears.

Another influence steadily at work on young girls is romantic fiction — short stories and novels. There have been several surveys to show that just as little girls are taught to behave in a conditioned way, so does the heroine in romantic fiction, in women's magazines, in romantic films and novels, set a pattern. In *Is This Your Life?*, edited by Josephine King and Mary Stott, the authors look at the images and attitudes of the media towards women, and how women are conditioned by these. Betty Friedan, in *The Feminine Mystique* did a survey of American women's magazines, and in Germaine Greer's *The Female Eunuch* there is a marvellously funny chapter (if it were not tragic) analysing the plots and characters in the romantic fiction of such writers as Georgette Heyer, Barbara Cartland and Lucy Walker (all bestselling authors). The heroine is always sweet, beautiful, unassured of her own abilities. The man is always strong, handsome, assured, successful. (He can be wicked.) He is always in a superior social position to that of the girl. He will love, protect, honour and cherish her for the rest of her life. She will follow him to the end of the world and sacrifice everything for him. The story always ends in a kiss and marriage.

Barbara Cartland has sold over 40 million copies of her books. The following is the closing phrase of one of her latest books, *Fire on the Snow:* 'His lips sought hers...his mouth, passionate, possessive, compelling, took her captive. She was his for all eternity.' As in fairy stories, 'they live happily ever after,' which, of course, is simply not true. One in four marriages in Britain is now ending in divorce. In America and Australia it is the same.

Imagine what a shock it is to a young bride when, having been brought up on these ideas, these promises of married bliss, after a courtship when she is waited on at parties, taken out, with money spent on her and car doors opened for her, she finds that, after marriage, it is she who must do all the waiting on, all the supporting. She must get up four or five times during a meal to set food and drink before her husband; she will give herself the smallest and scruffiest piece of meat; if two meetings or two sporting activities clash, she must give up hers and stay home to care for the children. She must listen to all the things that have gone wrong in the office, but anything that has gone wrong during her day, such as an overflowing washing machine, a fretful child, a dinner spoiled, is all so trivial, so much 'woman's work', so little a part of 'real life', that no one wants even to hear about it, let alone sympathise with her.

Far from being supported and cherished, it is she who must have the strength to stay at home, alone, with small, difficult children. It is she who must do the supporting and cherishing. What money is left over after household expenses will be spent on her husband's leisure-time activities, not on hers, for he is doing the 'real work'. He needs relief. Hers is not 'proper work'. It is this male attitude that housework is of no importance that is forcing women into the outside workforce. It is not the women's movement that is doing it.

To return to those deceptive women's magazines, in order to be modern, some girls in stories do now have careers, but in romantic fiction or popular type television programs, the girls always give up their careers. Alternatively, the career women are portrayed as villains of the story, aggressive, or a threat to a happy marriage. In practically any escape-type book — detective, adventure, thriller, or spy story — women are shown in supportive roles, doing the cooking, being typists, secretaries, wives or daughters of the main character. Or else they are the victims, being bashed up. They are strangled, raped, mutilated, tortured. They are sometimes the murderers. They are hardly ever the detectives.

As far back as Shakespeare in *The Merchant of Venice* women were giving up their careers for their men. Portia, that most successful woman barrister, says to her Lord Bassanio:

Myself and what is mine to you and yours
Is now converted. But now I was the lord
Of this fair mansion, master of my servants,
Queen o'er myself; and even now, but now,
This house, these servants, and this same myself
Are yours, my lord's.

Apart from portraying women in a passive and artificial role in their stories, the other contents of women's magazines reinforce the same role. Women are bombarded with articles telling them how to make their marriage a success, how to keep their husbands, how to keep their figures. Women are to be the givers, the reshapers of self, the adaptors, the sacrificial lambs. Daily attacked with such propaganda, how can they escape? Naturally they feel inferior. Ultimately they become inferior.

I can imagine two objections being raised here. Firstly, it may be accepted that girls do give up their careers, and do end up in the home, but you may say most of them are happy there. After all, someone has to go out and earn money, and someone has to stay home and look after children. There are, however, plenty of reports and surveys to show that the majority of women are not happy in the home. Many take to drugs and alcohol. It is specially hard for them when their children become teenagers and do not want or need their mothers any more. There is much less pressure and much less of a 'generation gap' in families where mothers have outside jobs or outside interests. There is also less pressure on a husband to succeed, or to be constantly paying his wife attention, where a wife has outside interests or an outside job.

Secondly, and here you would be right, you may ask, 'Is not the same pressure put on men to marry?' Many men also make bad marriages under pressure, but several things alleviate their plight. There may be pressure on a man who reaches the age of thirty unmarried, but at least he is not considered a failure. Rather he is an eligible bachelor, certainly a good escort. Further, if a man's marriage is a failure, he has his work as an antidote. He also has contacts and friends at work. His work informs him and increases his ability. He has someone to discipline him at work, that terrible boss.

A woman is confined to a home, where she can be desperately lonely. Her work is repetitive, monotonous, dirty, irritating, menial. She has no one to make her work, and what she does is destroyed, either eaten or untidied, almost as soon as she does it. A male clerk in a bank may find it monotonous dealing with columns of figures each day, but at least he has company, and at least yesterday's figures are still there. No one tears them up, nor does he have to start again on the same page of figures. He can see yesterday's figures or yesterday's report neatly there, and he can add to it.

Contrary to all common opinion, contrary to all those accepted myths about men being 'caught' in marriage, men actually gain more from being married than women, and, once again, there are many surveys to prove this.

These have been collected and discussed in a fascinating book, *The Future of Marriage,* by Dr Jessie Bernard. In it she says:

> ...men have been railing against marriage for centuries. If marriage were actually as bad for men as it has been painted by them, it would long since have lost any future it may have had. In the face of all the attacks against it, the vitality of marriage has been quite stupendous. Men have cursed it, aimed barbed witticisms at it, denigrated it, bemoaned it — and never ceased to want it and need it and to profit from it...contrary to all the charges levelled against it, the husbands' marriage, whether they like it or not (and they do), is awfully good for them.

To prove her point Dr Bernard quotes from a number of different sociological and psychological surveys. For example, most divorced men marry again. Widowed men are miserable. 'They show more than expected frequencies of psychological distress and their death rate is high.' One survey showed that death occurred early twice as often among widowed men as amongst widowed women.

Their suicide rate is also high, being the third ranking cause of death among widowed men. Another survey showed that married men lived longer than unmarried men. Not only do they live longer but they are happier. Yet another survey showed that twice as many married men as unmarried men reported themselves as very happy. Twice as many never-married men as married men reported themselves as not too happy. Married men were also more affluent, and in 1975 in Britain 47 per cent were receiving help from their wives in supporting the family and the number was increasing steadily. What's more, in the families where the women worked outside the home, the women showed fewer symptoms of psychological distress, which, in turn, benefited the husbands. She quotes from Paul Glick, who found that 'being married is about twice as advantageous to men as to women in terms of continued survival'.

The reverse side is that being married is not half as good for wives as for husbands. A number of different surveys on different aspects showed that more wives than husbands report marital frustration and dissatisfaction; more report negative feelings; more wives than husbands report marriage problems; more wives than husbands consider their marriage unhappy. Twice as many wives as husbands say that, given the opportunity, they would not marry the same person again. Wives report that their problems start sooner and last longer. Wives reporting no problems at all were far fewer than husbands who reported none. More married women than married men consider they are about to have a nervous breakdown; more experience physical and psychological anxiety; more have feelings of inadequacy in their marriage, and blame themselves more. Further, the health of married women compares just as unfavourably with unmarried *women* as it does with *married* men.

Yet another survey shows that more married than unmarried women are bothered by feelings of depression, are unhappy most of the time, dislike their jobs, sometimes feel they are about to go to pieces, are afraid of death, terrified by windstorms, worried about catching diseases, and bothered by pains and ailments in different parts of their bodies. The amount of crime committed by married women is greater than committed by unmarried women. Single women are better educated, have higher average incomes, and higher occupations than married women.

In another study, Aymond B. Willoughby said that either 'a calm type of women remains unmarried or...marriage had disturbing effects upon women'. Unmarried women show better health, better emotional adjustment and greater self-reliance, a greater sense of personal freedom and fewer withdrawing tendencies. He said that wives tend to 'dwindle' and to be less well able to take care of themselves.

Replies from both men and women show that women make

greater adjustments in marriage.

Working wives are overwhelmingly better off than housewives, complain of pains and ailments less, commit suicide less often, have fewer nervous breakdowns, in truth 'being a housewife makes most women sick'.

This has been a long chapter, but it is an important one, for the attitude of a young girl to marriage will affect and alter every aspect of her life — her education, her ability, her confidence, her ultimate happiness. I would therefore like to repeat that I am not particularly against marriage. I am just against girls thinking that marriage will solve all their problems and give them life-long happiness.

Ultimately I am sure there will be a number of marriage contracts drafted from which marrying couples can choose: contracts that will allow for the sharing of goods if marriages break down, taking into account the non-paid work that a wife has contributed while those goods have been acquired or a business built up; contracts that give a wife who stays at home a right to part of her husband's earnings; contracts which provide for men to share in household chores and the care of children.

Until then girls should realise they must prepare for a life and a career which may not include marriage or for a marriage that is only part of their life and a life that includes other interests and activities. They should discuss these things with their prospective husbands before marriage. They should not think that everything will just work out beautifully and that they will live happily ever after. Nor, of course, should they believe that such discussions will solve all problems, but at least they will give a young man a knowledge of what a young woman feels on these matters, and will give a young woman a chance to know how the man reacts to such suggestionsl It is much better to know the worst — and the best — before rather than after marriage.

SUGGESTIONS FOR OBSERVATION AND DISCUSSION

1 Make a list of advertisements on television and in other media that make marriage or housework appear glamorous. How many advertisments make it look realistic?

2 Make a note of remarks in conversations about a girl, after the age of twenty, not yet being married. Casually raise the subject in conversation with adults, and see what they say.

3 Observe and make notes of films, television programs, books, stories, and other writing, which portray a girl or woman giving up a project, a plan, a career, a day's outing or even an idea, to fit in with a man, and how often some such statement as 'following him to the end of the world' is made.

4 Observe and note how many films, stories, etc, end with a kiss between the male and the female.

5 Study women's magazines and see how much emphasis is placed on improving a woman's looks or figure or home-making ability. Discuss whether you feel this constant urging of women and girls to improve themselves must make them lose confidence in themselves, and feel they are less good and less capable people.

6 Note how often men put down their wives in public and at parties, contradict them, make them look foolish. Do you feel this must make a woman feel nervous about speaking and lose confidence in herself? Discuss whether this ultimately can result in her becoming a less able, thinking person.

7 Study films, books and television spy, adventure or murder stories, and note (a) how often the woman is shown in a supporting role; (b) how often she is the detective, the leader or the master spy.

6 MAN-MADE MYTHS

In spite of the many disabilities women suffer, such as lower aims for their education, the influences not to achieve, the loss of several years' training and experience due to childbearing, a frequent loss of confidence in their own abilities, and the difficulty of doing two jobs, more and more women are entering the workforce.

The figures show that in Britain in 1980 women's participation in the work force was 39.5 per cent. In 1901 this figure was 29.1 and in 1931 29.8 per cent. What is more, while in 1911 13.1 per cent of the female workforce was married, and in 1931 this figure had only increased to 15.2, in 1980 it had reached 67.6 per cent. Therefore married women made up 26.7 per cent of the total labour force. And in 1977 a survey done revealed that 89 per cent of women of working age had worked at some stage in their life. Quite staggering figures, I'm sure you'll agree. In Australia the latest government figures show similar patterns. Whereas in 1901 female participation in the total workforce was 21 per cent, in 1971 it was 32 per cent. In 1980 it was 35.86 per cent. More important still, in 1933 11 per cent of the female workforce was married, in 1971 this figure was 57 per cent, and in 1980 it had gone up to 66 per cent.

There are many reasons for this. Inflation and the increasing standard of living that people expect are causing more married women to work for economic reasons. Women are having smaller families, because of the pill and because they are beginning to realise they no longer have a duty to have large families. In fact, world population is growing at such a rate that there are many who preach against large families. Women are finding their useful child-rearing time is a very short part of their entire life span, which is increasing, and they need another occupation. Finally, with the increasing influence of feminism and women's liberationist ideas, women are beginning to resent their economic dependence, to gain strength from each other in the fight against their unequal status, and to be willing to admit that being a housewife does not fulfil them, develop them or use their full abilities. They are therefore seeking wider and more active roles in society. They are also finding, if they are willing to work and organise, that they can earn money.

Of course, because of their conditioning, their misuse of their educational abilities, and the fact that they still mainly run the house, do the housework as well as any outside job they undertake, they still usually end up in the supportive, lower-paid, least rewarding positions. The average full time woman worker's wage in both Britain and Australia is well below the average man's. In Britain in 1979, women's weekly earnings (including overtime) were equivalent to only 63.6 per cent of men's. In Australia in 1980 the average full-time woman worker's wage (including overtime) was $159.20 compared to the same for the average man (including overtime) of $235.20. Women have usually lost several years from the workforce, they have often lost confidence, and they lack the mobility of men. If offered a promotion in another city, they can seldom take it. Whole households are frequently moved for a man's job, but not for a woman's.

Nevertheless, they are returning to the workforce in large numbers (though in times of high unemployment men often get priority over women when jobs are filled). Unfortunately, in addition to all the disabilities mentioned above, there is one further very large and very subtle force at work against women. This force is the sum of many myths that are continually stated and accepted about women, myths that, by and large, are not true, and which constantly work against women getting the best position or positions appropriate to their abilities.

For example, girls are often not given promotion or not employed in a job because employers believe that girls will probably leave to get married. Yet a survey in 1973 showed that 19 per cent of single, widowed and divorced women had changed their jobs in the past 12 months, while the corresponding figure for males was 21 per cent. 13 per cent of married women had changed their jobs in this period, while the figure for males was 12 per cent. Very little difference, you will admit. And the evidence seems to show that people in more interesting, responsible work are more likely to stay in the job than those doing boring dead-end jobs.

Another common myth is that absenteeism is greater among women than men. In Britain in 1977 the General Household Survey indicated that absenteeism rates do not differ much for women and men; when the Survey was done, 6 per cent of women and 6 per cent of men were absent from work. In Australia a survey into absenteeism carried out by the Department of Productivity in 1977 showed that sex made no difference in attendance. The absentee rate for men and women were both 4 per cent. Absence from work seems to be related to the grade of work, not of the worker. The Department of Employment in Britain has stated that 'It need cause no surprise if the most monotonous, low-paid and low status jobs are those which show the highest absence rates; and if these jobs happen to be filled by women the fact will be reflected in the absence rates aggregated by sex'.

As women are usually in the most monotonous and least fulfilling jobs, the small difference is not relevant. Further, men who are honest about women employees (and there are many such men) admit that women overall are more reliable, dependable, take fewer long lunch hours, waste less time drinking with other men, etc.

Another myth that is held against women in business is that they are too 'emotional' to be given responsible positions. It is true that many women are 'emotional' in that they tend to become tearful when under stress, and we have discussed the reason for this earlier. Because girls have to suppress so many of their natural feelings, reactions, actions, and learn to behave artificially, in a ladylike, passive manner, feelings of frustration are built up inside them, and, because they cannot express these in honest anger (that would be unladylike), they show relief for these feelings in tears, which are considered feminine, ladylike, and acceptable.

So women in business do sometimes show their stresses by tears. But how do men show them? I have seen men under stress grow white with anger. I have seen them shake with anger and anxiety and nervousness. I have seen them reveal their anxiety and strain by aggressive anger, by berating their employees, by completely illogical attacks. But whereas if a woman reveals her stress she is

considered 'emotional', and therefore unfit for responsible positions, a man is excused as 'having had a bad day' or 'being under great strain' or even, maybe, 'his wife's giving him a bad time at home'. The same sort of excuse is seldom made for women. It is accepted that a man can be aggressive, bad tempered and bossy at work. It is even sometimes held to make him a better businessman. Such consideration is never given to a woman. All her faults and weaknesses are held up for inspection, analysis and criticism.

Which leads to yet another of those man-made myths, that when women are given authority in business they become aggressive. In fact, the whole of the women's movement is sometimes condemned because its followers are 'aggressive'. Some women in these situations undoubtedly are aggressive. They have often had to be aggressive to get there. If women had not tied themselves to fences back in the last century, women would not have the vote today. By the same token we would never have had the revolution in France or democracy in England or any of our liberties if someone sometime had not been aggressive.

But there are many women in authority who hold strong views and are not at all aggressive in their behaviour or their expression. Also, a woman has only to hold a view, or express it in ever so gentle a voice, that is against the common idea of what a woman's view or behaviour should be, to be considered by many as 'aggressive'. Anything that threatens accepted normal behaviour or accepted patterns of thought is considered by some people to be 'aggressive'.

Another general myth under which women suffer is that they are naturally suited for bringing up children and for home-making work, an attitude already discussed. This results in women, even in the professions, tending to be channelled into children's areas. Women doctors often become pediatricians (children's doctors). It is considered suitable for women in the home to take an active part in voluntary hospital work or work for children's homes, etc.

I suffered particularly in this direction. When I started to write, my father suggested I write children's books. It was not his fault. It was a common assumption of the day, and I was silly enough to follow his suggestion. But a children's author is never considered a 'real author' in the writing world. Had the same number of hours I spent researching, writing and getting published my twenty children's books been spent instead on writing well-researched, historical, factual books, a subject in which I am more interested than anything else, I would have had a worthwhile body of work to my name in the subjects in which I am most absorbed.

In the same way, when I started reviewing books for my father's journal, I was given the children's books to review. Similarly, there was never any thought that I would carry on the family business, although I worked in it, at every level, for so long. I managed it when my father went overseas. But when he came to retire, a young man took over his position. Again it was as much my fault as my father's. I am sure had I shown any wish or ambition or confidence in myself, or been willing to go against the attitudes of my friends that married women did not work, my father would have been willing to let me try. It would have been difficult, for in those days, believe it or not, it was quite usual for businesses to dismiss women when they married.

But luck intervened on my behalf again. When my youngest child was fourteen, I went back into the business, again in a supporting role, as an editor of one of the publications produced. About this time there was a major management re-shuffle and as a result the board of directors asked me to take over the business. There are many, many women as capable as I who are never given such an opportunity.

Another infuriating myth, if you happen to be a woman, is the one that women are hopeless about money. There is a constant stream of jokes, comic strips, cartoons and comments about women's stupidity with money. In actual fact most women are very good managers of money. In the average household they are given a limited amount of money for housekeeping and caring for and clothing the children, and they have to make it do. They also mostly spend far less money on themselves than men do. I am now often at expensive luncheons with men, whereas as a housewife I seldom lunched on more than a sandwich. Men spend more on their beer and their sporting pleasure than the average women does. Men usually spend more on their clothes, as they need them for their career. Excluded here, of course, are those women married to very wealthy men, women who have all the money they need for clothes and pleasure and help in the house. They are in a very small

minority, and actually lead a very unsatisfactory, if glamorous, life because they have given up their independence.

Another myth typical of man's attitude to woman is the criticism made of women drivers. If a woman makes a mistake while driving, one frequently hears the comment: 'Woman driver!' Yet statistics and surveys always show that women are better and safer drivers. If a man driver makes a mistake, no one says: 'Man driver!' They just think or say something like: 'That idiot'. Also, a woman driving with a man in the car is subject to a barrage of advice. This is acceptable behaviour, and woe betide a woman who gets annoyed. But if a woman makes any comment about a man's driving, she is labelled 'a back-seat driver'.

Similarly, women are always supposed to talk too much. Again there are many jokes about this. Admittedly, some women do talk a lot, but so do many men, and when men are lengthy talkers they can be utter, utter bores. But time any mixed conversation, and you will find men do the most talking. Admittedly, when women are in a group, they sound noisier. This is mostly because their voices are shriller, and, having to listen to men so much, when they get together they all tend to speak at once. Also the confidence they often lack in mixed company comes back in female company, and often causes them to talk too much.

That very common myth about men being 'caught' in marriage has already been discussed in full. In fact it is the women who are 'caught', well and truly, and the men who get most of the advantages.

One final typical myth is the attitude that women 'always get their own way' or are 'the boss'. Again the truth is different. Because men have the economic power, they make all the real decisions in marriage. Women automatically take on their husband's way of life, living in the city where his work is, adopting his sports, adapting themselves to his way of life. And if women often appear to 'get their own way', it is only because if a woman wants something badly against her husband's wishes, she has to argue, battle, wheedle or be downright beastly to get it. So it becomes a 'big deal', and it looks as if she is 'getting her own way'. When a woman is following a man's way of life, decisions or desires, it is done automatically, without making a fuss, and so makes no impression or is not noted.

Perhaps you will think I have gone on at some length about these myths, and that some of them are rather petty, and indeed some of them are. They are nevertheless extremely important, because they give an untrue picture of male-female relationships and an untrue picture of a woman's abilities. If people say these things often enough about women, it affects their opportunities to be given positions of responsibility. If repeated in many different ways, even women come to believe them. They then further lose their confidence in their capabilities.

SUGGESTIONS FOR OBSERVATIONS AND DISCUSSION

1 Bring up in conversation, particularly with adult men, the subject of whether women are suitable for management positions in business. Note the reasons that will be given for or against.

2 Listen to several mixed conversations and gauge the length of time that men talk compared to women.

3 Collect examples of jokes, cartoons, comic strips, etc which show women as being irresponsible about money. List some women you know who are (a) good money managers, and (b) unnecessarily extravagant.

7 THE DOUBLE STANDARD

Another disability under which women suffer continually is 'the double standard'. In other words, what is all right for men is all wrong for women. This constantly cripples the chances of a woman to achieve her full potential, and is equally crippling in taking away her confidence. If she is at all different from the accepted view of a female, she is conscious that people are being critical of what she does, and this makes her self-conscious and hesitant. Exactly the same actions are acceptable, excused, sometimes even praised in a man. This enables him not only to benefit from the freedom it gives him, but often also to 'hide behind a woman's skirt'. While he is taking advantage of his greater freedom, she, being so much more inhibited, is covering up for him, keeping the home fires going.

The best known and most obvious double standard is that related to sexual behaviour. Until fairly recently, and still in many cultures, it was, and is, considered all right for a boy or man to sow his wild oats sexually, but a girl had to be a virgin. This is changing now in many communities, but a girl will still be greatly criticised if she is considered too 'promiscuous', whereas a boy is considered 'a bit of a lad'.

In marriage, also, there are always excuses made for a husband who strays sexually, but a woman doing the same thing is considered greatly lacking in respectability. Although there is more tolerance today, there is still enough truth in these statements for women to suffer and be limited by them. Particularly in regard to children, a woman is considered an extremely bad mother if she neglects her family for a sexual experience. At the same time, if her husband does the same thing, she is expected, for the sake of the children, to stay at home, and take the place of both mother and father.

A far more subtle aspect of this sexual double standard is the way in which women are made to feel perpetually guilty about everything that goes wrong. This goes back to the story of Adam and Eve in the Bible, when Eve is blamed for the entry of sin into the world. Eve gives way to the temptations of the serpent and eats the apple forbidden by God, and then she, in turn, persuades Adam to eat it. As the biblical story of the creation of the world is no longer widely accepted, the theory of evolution now being generally believed, one wonders why adults read, and apparently accept, and make their children read, the biblical story of the Garden of Eden, and Adam and Eve's banishment from it.

One feels somehow that men feel guilty about sex. This, of course, is part of their upbringing and inhibitions, and they cannot be blamed for it. Generations of church and other teaching have attached guilt to sex, which is a great tragedy, sex being one of the greatest experiences in life. This being so, however, men do tend to feel guilty about sex, and to explain this, or lessen their feeling about it, they blame it on someone who should be their most beloved partner (and often is) — woman. You find many signs of this. There are the mothers and fathers who give their sons no other sex education than to be 'careful of those wicked women'. There are the enternal triangle stories and films where the person at fault is always 'the other woman', never the husband, who is 'led astray'. There is the fact that when a fourteen-year-old girl gets pregnant she is usually blamed, and not the boy involved. She should have shown greater strength.

The attitudes of many of those people who disapprove of pensions for unmarried mothers, or who disapprove of contraceptive knowledge or abortion, are founded on the basic fact that people believe women should be punished for sexual enjoyment. In some circles even a married woman who 'enjoys sex' is considered somewhat wicked. Many of these are extreme viewpoints, but they are still there among many people, and the lack of ability shown by most parents to give their children proper sex education is a sign of the guilt they feel about sex.

Not so extreme, in fact very general, is the attitude that women are to blame when their children do something wrong. It is a well-known joke about men that when their children do something good they are 'my' children, but when they do something bad they talk of them to their wives as 'your' children. Again, this is one of those things that to a woman is not funny at all. I bore the burden of guilt for every wrong thing my children did for many years. It was only after twenty-five years of marriage, and two years of feminist reading, that, when my husband complained about something my youngest son did, I finally had the sense to say: 'He's as much your child as mine. You stop him doing it. Perhaps if you'd spent more time with him when he was little, he might have been different. I did the best I could.'

It may sound petty, but it is very true. I did do the best I could. Women are left alone with their children all day and often during evenings as well, so if the children are not perfect, of course it's the result of the way the mother brought them up. But it's not their *fault*. Has anyone ever yet been able to solve the problem of how best to bring up children? It seems to me that the most satisfactorily brought up children are those where both parents take an equal part, but under our present system of marriage, and the division of work as it is, it hardly ever happens.

It is similar with working mothers. Over and over again one hears leading politicians, church leaders, or establishment type people

say, when they hear about delinquents: 'The trouble is all those mothers who go to work these days'.

Some women have always gone to work because they have had to, and they have not produced delinquents. There is absolutely no evidence whatsoever that working mothers produce delinquent children. There is evidence that many delinquents come from broken or unhappy homes, but these can be wealthy homes; or homes where the mothers and fathers are self-centred, selfish, at odds with each other; or homes where a mother is always alone, unhappy, neurotic, dissatisfied, with the husband constantly away; or homes with drunken parents.

A woman is perpetually made to feel guilty about something. A simple example is a family packing up to go away. 'What are you bringing all this stuff for?' asks the disgruntled husband, as he packs the car. As soon as the destination is reached the husband will be saying: 'Why didn't you bring that old brown coat of mine?'

A much less trivial example is when parents desert. When a man deserts his young wife, and maybe four or five children, because he cannot stand the strain any longer, men are critical, but they usually make some excuse, will often blame the wife, and the state looks after a deserted wife and children very poorly. But what if a wife walks out on a husband and several children? The average person is filled with horror at the mere thought of it. The woman is not only wicked, but positively unnatural. Yet the woman at home is subject to just as great pressures, often far greater, for she has no escape during the day, no relief from the drudgery and boredom of poverty and several young children.

A similar double standard is applied to drinking. It is accepted that men drink too much and it is permissible that they spend at least Friday night drinking with the boys. Women frequently stay sober at parties in order to drive their drinking husbands home. But the woman who drinks too much is subject to the greatest criticism.

A more subtle double standard is applied to a woman who makes a mistake, either small or large. 'Just like a woman,' people say. If a man makes a mistake, it is looked upon as merely a human error. The phrase 'Just like a man' means something quite different.

Yet another double standard concerns humour. Women are the constant butt of men's humour, in marriages, in business, in

entertainment, in cartoons, comic strips, films and books. Women have to grin and bear it. In fact, the feminist movement considers it one of their secret weapons. Men who are against the women's movement (fortunately not all are and many men have been leaders in the battles women have fought for equality) can never quite take women or their movement seriously. They do not really believe women will continue, and win, their fight for equality. They continue to think of it as a joke. But if women are a joke to men, just try making fun of a man. A man takes very unkindly to being made fun of — especially by a woman.

Another double standard is found in the attitude of men to women's work. They do not take it seriously. If it is housework it is not work at all. 'What do you do with yourself all day?' they ask the mother of three children. If it is an additional job outside the house, it is also not taken seriously. If there is any sort of family crisis, the women must give up her job. If the children are sick, she is to stay home. Again, there are notable exceptions to this, but generally speaking, a man will always put his work before a woman's. Also, if a woman is doing work at home, such as writing, she is constantly subject to interruptions, by her children and her husband. But no one interrupts a man. Not only does a wife not interrut him, even if he is only writing a personal letter, but she does not let the children interrupt him. 'Leave Daddy alone. Daddy is working. Don't interrupt him.'

Again, some of these examples may seem petty, but they indicate a general attitude that a woman is an inferior creature. Because this attitude is so widespread it lessens her opportunities to develop her full personality and ability, and it also lessens her opinion of herself. She finally believes them, and often acts according to them.

The final double standard, however, is in no way petty. This is the double standard of chivalry as compared to servitude. When one becomes involved in arguments about feminism or women's liberation, the most common question one gets asked by men is: 'But don't you like having doors opened for you? Don't you like being waited on?' And in arguments women say: 'But I don't want to be liberated. I like to have men wait on me. I like to have doors opened.'

This is what I call the 'door-opening' double standard. And apart from its being so thoroughly petty (what's so important about having a door opened? I rather like opening doors), it represents such a terrible double standard and is such an example of complete hypocrisy that it is almost unbelievable that people can still think this way.

The same man who says he puts a woman on a pedestal, and wants to open doors for her, to be chivalrous towards her, is quite happy to let her wait on him in the evenings, no matter how tired she is from caring for children all day. He lets her do menial, dirty, heavy tasks such as scrubbing floors, washing dirty nappies, hanging heavy sheets on the line, mopping up after sick or dirty children.

Another side of the hypocrisy in this attitude is that, far from being chivalrous towards women, many men in fact despise them. They certainly think them inferior. Have you noticed how people trying to criticise some man for some action will use a female description? A man is said to be 'just like an old woman' or 'as silly as a girl'. Actually many old women are extremely fine, efficient, capable women, far more so than many old men.

If you want to read of some of the worst ways men describe women, and show their contempt for them, read Germaine Greer's *The Female Eunuch* or the opening chapters of Kate Millett's *Sexual Politics*. Many famous authors such as Ernest Hemingway showed a complete contempt for women.

The same hypocrisy is shown by men in sexual attitudes towards women. Conservative men will tell a dirty or sexual joke at a dinner party, but will be shocked at a woman demanding that contraceptives should be advertised openly or sold from machines. When women started standing up at political meetings and asking politicians for sex education in schools, and more birth-control clinics, people started talking about 'those awful women'. Some politician said, 'They can't talk about anything but sex', saying this was most 'unfeminine'.

What a ridiculous double standard! The sexual act, in which practically everyone takes part, which is, after all, spelt out in marriage ceremonies as one of the reasons for marriage, *must not be talked about*. It is all a secret. *Nice* women do not talk about these things. I sometimes wonder what this type of man thinks goes on in a woman's head during the sexual act. Does she go into a state of nothingness? Does her mind go blank? Does she not know what is happening? How can such people believe it is wrong to discuss what is after all one of humanity's most widely practised activities.

Again, many of you will accuse me of exaggerating. I wish I were. Many people think the way I do, and believe in honest discussion, but there is still no official sex education in British and Australian schools. It is left to each individual school, and you should observe what happens in some schools as soon as sex education is discussed, and note the opposition it receives. There are still doctors who are unsympathetic when girls and women go to them for sex and contraceptive advice, and even some who will not give this advice. Abortion in Britain and Australia is still not a matter of choice for a woman, but only allowed if she can prove a pregnancy would harm her physically or mentally, or that there is a risk of injury to the physical and mental health of her existing children, or if there is any substantial risk that if the child were born it would be seriously physically or mentally handicapped. Even then it is not allowed in some parts of Australia, and the hardly won gains that have been made are constantly under serious attack in both Britain and Australia.

And, of course, it is particularly the girl or the woman who suffers through this terrible lack of free sexual discussion, proper information and inhibition against sex education, because it is she who becomes pregnant as a result of a sexual act. She may become emotionally involved beyond her intention, and also face the situation of an unwanted pregnancy. Her upbringing may make this problem especially difficult to beat.

It has been said that if men and women bore children in turn, there would never be more than three children in any family, the woman having the first, the man the next, and the woman the third. Another joke, but also terribly true. And few men would put up with the misery, the sacrifices, the upset plans, the inconveniences, the deprivation that an *unwanted* pregnancy brings — though there is no greater joy than a *wanted* pregnancy.

Apart from anything else, it is such a 'head in the sand' attitude, because countless young girls every year get pregnant, and, unfortunately, it is often the nicest and most loving girls — and wives — to whom this happens. The young girl who 'sleeps around' will usually be prepared, but the well-intentioned young girl who finds herself emotionally involved, and carried beyond her depth, either is not prepared or feels it will indicate some lack in her feeling for a boy or a man if she introduces the need for care or prevention.

These pregnancies in young girls often lead to forced marriages and misery for the girl, the boy, and worst of all, the children. Statistics show that the early breakdown of so-called 'shot-gun' marriages is quite overwhelming. This is one of those wrong reasons for getting married, yet the alternatives are also terribly hard for a girl.

Any young girl who has not received proper sex education either at home or school should arm herself with a book on the subject — there are several titles in the book list at the back of this book. *Our Bodies, Ourselves* by Angela Phillips and Jull Raleusen (Penguin 1979) is an invaluable book, with information on health, anatomy, sexuality, relationships, nutrition, exercise, venereal disease, contraception, childbearing, parenthood, self-defence, menopause, rape and many other subjects.

Nearly all these examples of the double standard exist because the relationship between men and women is unequal. The double standard works to the man's advantage because it enables him to get away with so much. He can behave badly because his wife covers up for him. He can afford to be sanctimonious and unbending about sex education and birth control, because he does not suffer from it in the same way. He can force the double standard because he is economically in charge. He has the final say.

This whole situation leads to many miseries in marriage and in male-female relationships. The woman who is thus dominated takes it out on her man in many ways by jealousy, unkindness, frigidity, meanness, pettiness. This leads to much basic antagonism between men and women, to many broken unhappy relationships within marriage, to many broken marriages. What a tragedy it is!

A good sexual relationship is one of the most exciting, wonderful experiences that exist, and when this is combined with a genuinely deep feeling and respect for the partner in that relationship it becomes so much richer. When this, finally, is combined with the sharing of the bearing and bringing up of children no more perfect relationship can exist.

If all the double standards, the domination, the dependence and the lack of understanding and honest discussion could be done away with, a woman would become equal to a man. If both could share in all the bad as well as the good things in marriage, both men and women could have so much to gain. To quote Margaret Mead, that great anthropologist:

...to the extent that either sex is disadvantaged, the whole culture is poorer, and the sex that, superficially, inherits the earth, inherits only a very partial legacy...we must think instead of how to live in a two-sex world so that each sex will benefit at every point from each expression of the presence of two sexes.

SUGGESTIONS FOR OBSERVATIONS AND DISCUSSION

1 Collect examples of actions it is all right for a man to do, but for which a woman gets criticised. Bring casually into conversation the behaviour of men and women in regard to different things such as drunkedness, desertion, sexual behaviour, and see the different reactions you get.

2 Collect examples of women being blamed for rape, for children going wrong or misbehaving, or for marriages breaking down.

3 Start a conversation about women's liberation and see if the opening of doors, being waited on, or chivalry are brought up. Ask how this ties in with men allowing women to do such menial, hard tasks in the house.

4 Find out what sex education there is in the schools with which you are connected. If there is none, ask why, and see what reactions you get.

8 WHAT ARE THE SOLUTIONS?

Whatever the solutions are, they will not be easy, and they will not be quick, or there would be no need for a book like this. Probably they fall into two categories.

The first and the easiest, though it will be difficult enough, will be legislation, laws to do away with the greatest discriminations. In Britain and Australia, there are equal pay and sex discrimination acts, which, despite loopholes, are an important beginning, and should be extended and strengthened.

Among other laws that could be passed would be allowance for several different marriage contracts that young people could discuss and from which they could choose. There should be some type of legislation giving a wife a share of her husband's income (difficult as it will be to work it out), so that the woman who stays at home and works for no money has some power by right, over the family purse decisions. Married women should have the same pension rights as men. At the moment they are treated as dependants of their husbands and get lower pensions whether or not they are the chief breadwinner of the family or equal contributors to the family budget.

There should be good and plentiful child care centres so that women who want to can go out to work. Maternity leave benefits could be better. There should be proper state insurance schemes for pregnancy and legal obligations on employers to keep women's jobs open for them. At the moment these are mainly provided in the nationalised industries or in government bodies.

These are some of the things that feminist political groups are working for in all countries. They may sound impossible but much has already been achieved. Groups have campaigned for better maternity benefits, child care facilities, for fairer pension and welfare rights for women and on many other issues. Feminist groups had a powerful influence on the campaigns which eventually led to the equal pay acts and the sex discrimination acts.

But all the legislation in the world will not alter the situation until attitudes are changed. It is no good, for example, having marriage contracts which provide for the sharing of household chores and the caring of children, if girls are so anxious to get married that they do not ask for or want these things.

All the discussions and contracts in the world on the subject of shared housework will have no effect if men refuse to co-operate. Women will continue to be in a position of finding it easier to do a thing themselves than to keep reminding their husbands that they promised to do it.

It is no good a wife having some of her husband's earnings by law if he then refuses to give her any more. The wives to whom husbands give practically nothing will be better off, but financial matters in marriage will always be a matter of agreement between husband and wife. Real equality will never be achieved until girls learn to want it, and to discuss it, or demand it.

Similarly, in the business world, although equal pay has done a tremendous amount to help women economically, they will still not achieve their full potential while men refuse to promote them because of beliefs that women are not as good as men, are emotional, are liable to leave, or will stay away more than men.

In other words, the second and most difficult solution is the changing of attitudes: changing the attitude of girls, and women towards themselves, and changing the attitude of men and particularly of those in authority towards women.

This changing of attitudes will be a long, long task, and a difficult one, for women as well as men have to be persuaded. We have seen what conditioning does to girls and women, and this starts from the cradle. The majority of women bring up their sons to expect the same attention from their wives as their mothers have given them. The majority of women teach their daughters to seek happiness and fulfilment in marriage, not caring to see their own clearly. Men, with so many obvious advantages, will find it hard to give up their position of power in the workforce and privilege in the home.

In the long run it is young people, particularly the girls, who will make the changes and the decisions about their future, which is why I have written this book.

Girls must see their future as similar to that of boys. A girl must make sure she obtains a good education, good qualifications, and that she does not marry just for the sake of marrying. She must realise that decision-making comes from economic power, and she must plan to give herself economic equality. She must understand the importance of herself as an individual, as a person of importance in her own right. She must preserve her own personality, not allow society to sap her confidence, and not allow her reading and conditioning to make her believe marriage is her only goal.

It will not be easy. She will find herself teased, bullied, sometimes rejected. She will have to be persistent in her ambitions, resist many pressures, see her future clearly, not sacrifice her career for that of her boy friend, not devote so much time to attracting men, and make herself capable of standing on her own. She must learn to understand her body, and learn that 'love' is a relationship in which a man wants her for her personality as much as for her looks, has a deep understanding of her problems, a respect for her views, and a willingness to share the house and family chores with her.

The words of Helen Reddy's famous song, I am Woman, should be engraved on every young girl's heart:

You can bend but never break me
'cause it only serves to make me
More determined to achieve my final goal.
And I come back even stronger,
Not a novice any longer,
'cause you deepened the conviction in my soul.

As for boys, it too will take a long, long time to change their attitudes. The boy, and the man, must learn that he too will benefit by giving up his power and his privilege, by sharing and organising work so that both sexes take part in the important positions and in the decisions in life, and that he will be happier if his woman is happier and more fulfilled. To return again to Helen Reddy:

I am woman, watch me grow,
See me standing toe to toe,
As I spread my loving arms across the land.
But I'm still an embryo
With a long, long way to go
Until I make my brother understand.

9 A FINAL WORD FOR GIRLS

I would like to finish this book with a final word for girls, for it is a responsibility to write as I have written in these pages.

If, by any chance, any of you are influenced by my remarks, and find yourselves at the age of forty or so feeling lonely, without a husband or children, because you have perhaps put you career before some relationship, or because you have failed to compromise or conform, please do not blame me.

I am only expressing my own views and convictions. I am personally glad I am married, and I get a lot of joy and pleasure from my children, but I have many, many friends in the women's movement who have not married, or have no children, but who love their freedom, and are just as happy as I am.

If you do not marry, and do ever feel lonely, remember that there is no lonelier person than a wife and mother alone in a house with small children, or who is neglected by her husband or her grown children, or who finds herself, when she grows older, with no identity and no job in life.

Also, if you do join the band of feminists, you will find a wealth of friends and some wonderfully close relationships. Do not think there are no arguments or disagreements in the women's movement. With such a revolutionary aim as changing society, there are bound to be many different ideas about how to achieve it. Underneath all the different views, however, is a great community of women, with the same experiences, feelings and aims. To take one final quote from Helen Reddy, who writes such moving feminist songs because she knows what it is all about:

I am woman, hear me roar
In numbers too big to ignore,
And I know too much to go back to pretend,
'cause I've heard it all before
And I've been down on the floor,
And no-one's gonna keep me down again.

10 READ ON

There have been many books written on feminism — most, unfortunately, on a fairly academic level. The following are a few that for historical or personal reasons I have found particularly interesting and should like to recommend:

Carol Adams and Rae Laurikietis, *The Gender Trap,* Virago Quartet 1976. An excellent three part series for school children, their parents and teachers, analysing the expected behaviour and accepted sex roles of men and women in our society. The first book looks at education and work, the second at sex, love and marriage, and the third deals with messages and images we receive from language, humour, the media.

Simone de Beauvoir, *The Second Sex,* Penguin 1972. First published in 1949, this is one of the most brilliant and revealing studies of woman in all her aspects ever written.

Jessie Bernard, *The Future of Marriage,* Souvenir Press 1973. This is another brilliant book, giving a true and analytical picture of marriage and the way it disadvantages women.

Bruno Bettelheim, *The Children of the Dream,* Paladin 1971. Showing the way children are brought up communally in a kibbutz in Israel, it suggests they have greater security and fewer social problems than other families, although not necessarily achieving as much.

Anna Coote and Tes Gill, *Women's Rights. A Practical Guide,* Penguin 1978. A very comprehensive book, a mine of information on the laws and regulations which affect women and the means by which women can defend and extend their rights.

Jane Cousins, *Taking Liberties: An Introduction to Equal Rights,* Virago 1979. This kit is about equality in the eyes of the law, and shows how people's legal rights permeate not only their public lives but also their social, emotional and sex lives. Written for students from 14 upwards, it's packed with concise information and is entertainingly and wittily presented.

Eva Figes, *Patriarchal Attitudes: Women in Society,* Virago 1978. An excellent book showing how men, through religion and marriage, have kept women and their property within their power. It poses an alternative means of bringing up children outside marriage.

Betty Friedan, *The Feminine Mystique,* Penguin 1973. Written in 1963, this was the first of the modern books on the subject. It not only draws attention to women's inequality, but also analyses the ways in which girls and women are conditioned *not* to achieve, from birth, and the confusion suffered by girls who have been educated and do not know why or for what. One of the easier books to read and specially recommended.

Germaine Greer, *The Female Eunuch,* Paladin 1971. Possibly the book that most brought women's liberation into the public eye, it brilliantly analyses conditioning, the way men think of women, what marriage does to women, and feminism generally.

John Stuart Mill, *On Liberty, Representative Government, The Subjection of Women,* Oxford University Press 1912. Written in 1869 by one of the greatest thinkers of all time, this is a classic book on the inequalities to which women were and are subject, with a strong argument for their equal ability.

Kate Millett, *Sexual Politics,* Virago 1977. A famous but rather bitter book, it shows the contempt with which most men really hold women, and the way they exploit them.

Julia O'Faolain & Lauro Martines, *Not in God's Image,* Virago 1979, is a collection of extracts from contemporary writers on the position of women in European society throughout history. It adds a whole new dimension to the study of history.

Adrienne Rich, *Of Women Born,* Virago 1977 is an imaginative blend of memoir and history, a view of women's role as mother throughout · history which draws on anthropology, medicine, history, literature and psychology. No one will feel the same about motherhood after reading this book.

Henry Handel Richardson, *The Getting of Wisdom,* Heinemann Educational, 1960.

Michael Rutter, *Maternal Deprivation Reassessed,* Penguin 1975. This shows that children are not necessarily deprived if their mother does not rear them, though some permanency in substitutes is necessary.

Elaine Showalter, *A Literature of Their Own,* Virago 1978. This is a study of British novelists from the 1800s to the present day — their lives, their writings, the world of fiction they created — including not only famous names such as George Eliot, Virginia Woolf, Jane Austen, but many less well-known and equally fascinating contemporaries.

Mary Wollstonecraft, *A Vindication of the Rights of Women,* Penguin 1975. Just to prove that women have not only recently started to complain about their predicament, this plea for equality was written in 1792.

Virginia Woolf, *A Room of One's Own,* Penguin 1974. First published in 1929, this short book is a sort of thinking aloud about why women have not reached equal status with men; it reaches the conclusion that it is because of physical disabilities and lack of encouragement.

SEX EDUCATION

A.C. Andry and S. Schepp, *How Babies are Made,* Time-Life 1968. A highly original and popular picture book treatment of sex and reproduction which has been used successfully with quite young children from about three upwards. Illustrated with coloured photographs of paper sculpture.

Jane Cousins, *Make It Happy,* Virago 1978. Written with the help of teenagers, their parents and teachers, it explains what sex is all about. Full of accurate information, and emotionally honest, frank and reassuring, it shows how sex can be something to be shared, enjoyed and understood.

Per Holm Knudsen, *How a Baby is Made,* Collins 1973. For really young children, with basic, honest information.

P. Mayle, illus. A. Robins, *What's Happening to Me?,* Macmillan 1976 and *Where Did I Come From?,* Macmillan 1978. The former is a guide to puberty for 9-13 year olds, sensitively written with delightful illustrations. The preface says 'This book is for all of you who are suffering from growing pains. We hope it brings some fast relief'. The second title is aimed at younger children, presenting the facts of life without any nonsense or evasion.

Angela Phillips & Jill Rakusen, *Our Bodies, Ourselves,* Penguin 1979. An extremely important book, it gives a great deal of valuable information on all aspects of women's health and sexuality; it covers anatomy, sexuality, relationships, nutrition, exercise, health, venereal disease, contraception, parenthood, childbearing, menopause, self defence, rape and many other topics. It is written in such a way that women can learn about their bodies, and so have more control over them and their lives. It includes personal accounts of various experiences.

Claire Rayner, *The Body Book,* Whizzard/Deutsch. This nicely designed, well-written book for the under tens deals with subjects difficult to explain: what taste and smell are, what causes hiccoughs and burps. There are sections on conception as well as growing old and dying.